GUARDIAN ANGELS

Susan Smitten

GHOST
HOUSE

Ghost House Books

The Publisher: Ghost House Books
Distributed by Lone Pine Publishing

10145 – 81 Avenue	1808 – B Street NW, Suite 140
Edmonton, AB T6E 1W9	Auburn, WA 98001
Canada	USA

Website: http://www.ghostbooks.net

Library and Archives Canada Cataloguing in Publication
Smitten, Susan, 1961–
    Guardian angels / Susan Smitten.

    ISBN 1-894877-59-4

    1. Guardian angels. I. Title.
BF1275.G85S64 2004   133.9   C2004-903936-9

Photo Credits: Every effort has been made to accurately credit photographers.
Any errors or omissions should be directed to the publisher for changes in
future editions. The images in this book are reproduced with the kind permission of the following sources: Corbis Images (p. 24, 75); Istock (p. 40, 64:
Fanelie Rosier; p. 49: Lidian Neeleman; p. 102: Mayr Budny; p. 145: Jack
Tzekov; p. 158: Carolyn Mckendry; p. 162: Matjaz Slanic; p. 170: Jessica Jones;
p. 216: Jan Bily); Library of Congress (p. 99, 110: HABS,PA,46-VALFO.V,2-8)

The stories, folklore and legends in this book are based on the author's collection of sources including individuals whose experiences have led them to
believe they have encountered phenomena of some kind or another. They are
meant to entertain, and neither the publisher nor the author claims these stories represent fact.

We acknowledge the financial support of the Government of Canada through
the Book Publishing Industry Development Program (BPIDP) for our publishing activities.

PC: P5

For my daughter, Naia.

It is this belief in a power larger than myself and other than myself which allows me to venture into the unknown and even the unknowable.
—Maya Angelou

Contents

Acknowledgments

This book came together with the help of so many people, mainly those whose stories fill these pages. There are some additional mentions that must be made: first to Shane Kennedy, whose luminous vision set this all in motion; to Maya Massar for generously sharing her knowledge and energy and opening my eyes to the realm of the "Winged Ones"; to Heather Anderson of British Columbia's Ghosts and Hauntings Research Society and Matthew Didier of the Ontario GHRS for their wonderful support in soliciting stories; to Rowena of Castleofspirits.com and Jeff Belanger of Ghostvillage.com and to the Goth By Nature website for opening their online discussion forums to my search for material and for permission to access people or reprint material; to my editors Chris Wangler, Gary Whyte and Rachelle Delaney, whose skill and sensitivity show on every page, as well as the rest of the incredible Ghost House gang, who are always there when needed; to the myriad of friends who believed in me and supported me; and to those whose stories did not make it into this collection but who know that it in no way diminishes the validity of their experience. I offer my deepest thanks to all who contributed to this book.

Introduction

A seer once told me that I am surrounded by spirits. At the time, I applied his comments directly to my personal circumstances, which were strained at best, and didn't consider the implications in the bigger picture. But when I came to write this book and reflected on the times in my life when I heard, saw or felt a spirit's presence, I remembered receiving comfort or vital information on several occasions. My experiences suggest that the spirits have been actively helping me throughout my life.

One of my first encounters occurred while on holiday in Jamaica during my second year of university. I was in my early 20s and traveled south with my boyfriend of the time for a ten-day respite from Ottawa's miserable, snow-clad winter. We rented a car and drove from our beach resort through the mountains to Kingston for a day of sightseeing. The trip to Jamaica's capital made us think that perhaps it would have been wiser to hire a driver. We negotiated narrow, hairpin turns in a small, standard-transmission car set up with right-hand drive (the Jamaican driving system is modeled after Britain's). I quickly learned to drive on the left-hand side of the road while seated in the right-hand side of the car.

We left Kingston for the return trip home later than planned and, as if things weren't bad enough, we soon found ourselves driving in the dark with extremely dim headlights to illuminate the road ahead. I had driven the majority of the way to Kingston, so it was now my boyfriend's turn at the wheel. Suddenly, as we rounded one very tight corner, a car with no headlights on raced toward us on our side of the road. The roads were narrow, and only a short, brick retaining wall separated us from a massive drop down a craggy cliff to the ocean hundreds of feet below. My boyfriend reacted to the sight of the other driver by pulling as far he could to the left, toward the cliff edge. I heard the paint scraping off my passenger door. And in the split second that it took for all this to happen, I heard a deep, male voice in my head say very clearly, "Don't worry. This isn't your time." I immediately relaxed. I didn't brace myself or scream. I just sat there. The other driver managed to avoid us by swerving hard, and just nicked our front bumper. He didn't stop, but fishtailed up the road and kept going. We sat frozen in our seats. My boyfriend finally uncurled his fingers from the steering wheel. When he found his voice, he asked me, "Why didn't you react? How could you stay so calm?" I thought it would sound ridiculous to reply, "Because I heard a voice in my head that said everything would be okay." Instead, I opted to lie and say that since it all happened so fast, I froze.

Years later, my second unusual encounter also took place on the road. This time, I was alone and driving home late at night on treacherous winter roads in Edmonton, Alberta. For reasons now unimportant, I was in a hurry. Add to that my notorious "lead foot" and it's safe to say my speed exceeded the posted limit by at least 15 miles per hour. Worse yet, my thoughts distracted me and I really wasn't "in" the car mentally. What happened next is difficult to explain. As I sped up a hill toward a big S-curve, all of a sudden the road in front of me disappeared and I saw myself hit the curb, flip my little Toyota Tercel and roll it several times. What I saw out the windshield was not the current reality but some future one. I responded to the vision as if it was real by instantly hitting the brakes. My car slid around the corner, where a fallen light standard lay across the road. I skidded to a stop inches from the gray metal post. My fingers practically cramped as they gripped the steering wheel. All I could think was, "What just happened? What *was* that?" After I calmed down, I had to put the car in reverse and drive in a lane of oncoming traffic to get around the fallen light. I realized as I drove the rest of the way home—much more slowly—that had I taken the corner at that speed, I probably would have hit that pole or swerved into the curb to try to stop. Was my life-saving vision an unexpected moment of clairvoyance or a major intervention from a guardian angel? I felt that *something* had stepped in, and I never shook the feeling that a protective spirit kept me safe that night.

When I thought about the experience, I wondered, "What do I really know about guardian angels? What is the difference between a guardian angel and a spirit guide or guardian spirit?" In researching the concept, I learned that the role of angels as personal guardians is an extremely popular belief in the collective human consciousness, both past and present.

The three major world religions—Christianity, Judaism and Islam—all accept the existence of angels. The Koran states, "For every soul, there is a guardian watching it." The ancient Romans believed that each family received protection from guardian spirits called Iares. According to the *Encyclopedia of Angels,* many other ancient cultures also named their guardian spirits: the Pakistani and Burmese called these beings *Nats,* Islam believed that the *Malaika* protected mankind and the Zoroastrians called their guardian angels *Fravashi.*

Several saints, such as Joan of Arc, saw angels. Socrates believed he had a guardian angel and often consulted it for advice. Guardian angels appeared to famous military leaders like George Washington and adventurers such as South Pole explorer Sir Ernest Shackleton and Mount Everest climber Francis Sydney Smythe. In *A Book of Angels,* Sophie Burnham quotes Smythe's 1933 account of his ascent and the angel that assisted him: "In its company I could not feel lonely, neither could I come to any harm. It was always there to sustain me on my solitary climb up the snow-covered slabs."

By the fourth century, winged angels—to set them apart from other beings like apostles—began appearing in art. Authors and poets, from Dante and Shakespeare to Edna St. Vincent Millay and William Wordsworth, included references to angelic beings in their works. And it was only a matter of time before Hollywood cashed in on the craze, with films like *Heaven Can Wait, Angels in the Outfield* and, of course, the Christmas classic *It's a Wonderful Life,* in which a lovable angel named Clarence saves down-trodden George Bailey from jumping off the Bedford Falls Bridge.

Many images of guardian angels, which I remember well from Saturday morning cartoons, depicted two beings, one good and one bad, perched on either shoulder. Catholic children often learned that they were each born with two guardian angels who would whisper advice, and it was up to the child to choose which voice to follow. Thomas Aquinas, however, endorsed the theory that only one angel watches over each person. He wrote that the tenure of the guardian angel begins at birth and continues throughout the person's life. While that remains the most popular view, some people believe that each individual is surrounded by an entourage of spirit guides and guardian angels.

More recently, various polls suggest a growing number of people believe in guardian angels. In his book *In Search of Angels,* David Connolly cites a 1992 Gallup Youth Survey that found 76 percent of American teen-agers aged 13 to 17 believe in angels, up from 64 percent in 1978. *Where Angels Walk* author Joan Wester Anderson quotes another Gallup poll that suggests nearly two-thirds of Americans believe in angels. An Associated Press art-icle entitled "An Age for Angels—Spiritual, Commercial Interest in Heavenly Beings on the Rise" notes, "Angels are turning up in people's lives with increasing frequency, and people are more receptive to the heavenly beings than ever before." Why the newfound resurgence in accepting angels? Perhaps humans embrace the belief in angels to counter the frightening or unexplainable aspects of life. After all, what could be more comforting and reassuring than to believe in a being, more powerful and somehow connected to the divine, which cares for and protects us as we plod our way through the minefields of life?

It seems to me that many people use the term "guardian angel" to refer to just about any sort of protective or guid-ing spirit. Some of the confusion may come from the Greek origin of the word "angel," *angelos,* which means messenger. Since people who experience a guardian angel or spirit generally receive important messages of guidance, one might assume that angels and spirits are one and the same. Is there a distinction? In *Ghosts, Spirits and Hauntings,* Patricia Telesco says that though they may appear similar, a fairly simple distinction separates guardian angels and spirit guides. Essentially, angels have never been human, whereas spirit guides have existed in human form. "Spirit guides can be anyone from a deceased relative to a master teacher," Telesco writes. Angels, beings of a semi-divine nature, are rarely visible but are often sensed as present, especially in times of great danger. Many of the stories I collected for this book tell of people who have felt an invisible buffer between themselves and serious harm. Guardian angels and spirit guides do, however, share a common function: to guide and protect, inspire and instruct.

To sort out my many questions, I sought the advice and wisdom of Maya Massar. Maya studied with various alternative healers and worked for many years as a natural healer and shaman. She has also seen, heard and felt angelic presences since she was a child. Ten years ago, she decided to integrate the two aspects of her life and offer "angel readings" to help others connect with their personal guardian angels. In a very personal message, her own angels instructed Maya to use her ability to facilitate the meeting of humans and angels. She practices near Vancouver, British Columbia, and offers individual readings and workshops to teach people how they can communicate with their angels. Maya explained to me that everyone has between one and nine personal guardian angels, but in her experience, most people have between three or five.

Maya describes angels as beings of "infinite love and light" that bring comfort, power and transformation. She says that we should understand the difference between a being that is of infinite love and light and one that isn't. People trying to connect to angels often get nervous and worry that they might conjure up a devil or a bad spirit, but Maya insists that connecting with angels is as simple as saying, "Angels be with me." Maya confirmed that the difference between guardian angels and guardian spirits is that the former have never taken human form. In fact, she says, the angels refer to humans as "the Courageous Ones" because, unlike them, we chose to live here on earth in human form to experience limitation and autonomy. Maya thinks of personal guardian angels as a "light family" because they are committed to specific humans throughout their lifetimes. They will also accompany those who believe into other lifetimes.

A definite difference exists between guardian angels and people who have passed on but choose to stay in light form to protect others. However, there is an element of semantics to the issue. Maya points out that if someone calls his deceased grandfather or dog his guardian angel, he means that this being loves him, watches over him and protects him, all of which is true. Such spirits can be viewed as guardian angels. Calling a deceased relative a guardian angel simply reflects how that person feels about the relative and how the relative feels about that person. In Maya's experience, a loved one who has passed on often remains present in spirit, usually until the living person is ready to let go of the loved one. That may take a whole lifetime, but when the time comes to let go, the spirit will no longer hover around. It will come if called, but will not be present like a personal guardian angel.

How do you know that the messages you receive are from your angel and not just something you made up or already knew? It's a tough distinction to make. Maya says that with practice, and by tuning in to the angels' presence, the distinction becomes more clear. Some people would call such an experience a product of intuition or coincidence. "If you want to call it intuition, that's fine," Maya says. "If you want to call it some kind of magical interaction or biochemical thing in your brain or guardian angel or voice of God, the angels don't care. But if you say 'I'm calling on my intuition to figure this out,' and can't figure it out, they can't help you. If you say 'I'm calling on my guardian angels,' and stay receptive, they can help you. So it's really just a choice."

How then do you call your guardian angels? It seems simple enough. Anything from a thought to a voiced request will work. Speaking out loud produces the best results because it expels the person's being into the air. According to Maya, that is the quickest way to get a guardian angel's attention. She offers a basic "prescription" to connect with angels, which involves four essential elements: a special place, a regular time, a ritual call and a simple question or task.

To start, set up a particular place that feels tranquil— your bed at night or a space in the house or in the garden. Intention is a large part of this exercise. The goal is to create an open, safe and sacred space, a peaceful, private refuge where you can be in communion with yourself. That space will begin to hold your energy. When your space is ready, pick a regular time to meet—or at least be open to meeting—with your guardian angels. Pick a time you can commit to, and whether it is once a month or once a day, show up. Don't commit to something that can't be honored because, as Maya explains, the guardian angels will come to expect regular visits and actually prepare for them. At the appointed time, have paper or a journal handy to note whatever experiences, or lack thereof, occur. Maya recommends showering and wearing clothes that allow for feelings of openness and safety.

For the ritual of calling the angels, Maya suggests using the four elements: fire, water, earth and air. It can be as simple as lighting a candle, touching a bowl of water, holding a stone and breathing as you say out loud, "I call on my angels to be present." No special statement is any more effective than another. A simple "be with me" or "give me a sign" will open the channel to communication. Singing is also a good way to call guardian angels, even if you think your voice sounds more like a moose call than a melody. Simply sing one note, and think of it as an offering to make contact. Guardian angels do not judge with critical ears, as humans often do.

This is where the question or simple task comes in. Ask a very concrete and simple question. The simpler and more direct the question, the simpler and more direct the answer will be. If someone has a rather vague request such as for guidance in his life, he may find the response difficult to discern. If this is a whole new experience, keep your questions or tasks very narrow. Ask, for example, "should I wear the red socks or green socks?" Then be still and listen. Maya says most people fall into one of three categories: those who see, hear or feel a response. Some may see images or colors, with eyes open or closed. Others might hear something with either their literal ears or inner ears. The third group may sense a presence or feel some sensation. Take notes and write down everything you see, feel or hear. Maybe you'll receive nothing. Thank the angels anyway, blow out the candle and finish the session. If you immediately see a bright red book cover, that could be your answer. If you receive a clear answer, be prepared to honor it and follow through, even if it doesn't seem convenient. Keep track of what happens next, even if nothing occurs. Maya claims that if you perform this ritual regularly, you will soon be able to discern real messages from those you make up. As you gain confidence in the answers you receive, you can start to ask broader questions. Constant communion with angels, like anything else, takes effort, but Maya insists it is worth it because angels are a source of comfort, and they want to help us.

Consider this, though: when we invite guardian angels to participate actively in day-to-day life, our lives will invariably change. Issues we would rather leave hidden under the bed may be swept out and exposed. To choose to interact with angels is to choose healing, according to Maya, "because they say that our pain is the golden key to our own transformation." Working with angels is not an escape from emotions or issues, but it can be a way to confront such issues with loving support.

Many people first experience angels during crises. They might suddenly find the strength to lift a car off an injured child or they might witness a being who shows up to help, then disappears. Several stories in this collection fall into the crisis category, such as Janet MacLellan's experience in Mexico (as told in "Message in Mexico" later in this book). Maya has her own tale to tell.

"I had a tire changed by a being that evaporated, but he was as physical as anyone I've seen. I laugh at this because this is not how I see angels, but he showed up like something out of *Unsolved Mysteries*." Maya found herself stranded at about 4 AM in a desert in Southern California, with no one around for miles. She tried to change the tire herself but could not get the lug nuts to budge. She looked around and in the dawn light saw only the open desert and no one to assist her. She says, "I looked down the road and said, 'Somebody help me.' I turned back, and about 30 feet away from me there was a white car parked. This young man, about 22, with an absolutely pristine face, ice blue eyes, blond, blond, hair, a fitted white T-shirt, white pants and white shoes walks up and says 'Can I change your tire for you?' " The good-looking man changed the tire. Maya thanked him profusely and he answered, "You're very welcome." Maya recalls he had a twinkle in his eye. She put the tire wrench and jack in the back of her car and turned back around. The man and his car had disappeared. "Gone. There was nowhere for him to go. I was in wide-open desert."

She explains that when serious danger arises, people sometimes experience such interventions. If someone has a job to complete in this lifetime and is about to die or be seriously injured, an angel will pick her up, sometimes literally, and move her out of harm's way. In my case, an angel showed a little preview of the scene to come.

In some cases, the messenger—be it guardian angel or spirit guide—appears in a form that will not cause alarm, as if it senses that the frail human may crumple or run in the other direction if exposed to the awesome sight of an angelic being. As an example, a friend of mine shared a story with me about her father, a pragmatic Brit whose heart ailment finally required surgery. While lying in his hospital bed after a rather dramatic, life-saving operation, my friend's father woke to see his local minister sitting by his bed and holding his hand. Comforted by the minister's presence, he relaxed and began the long road to recovery. After being released from hospital, he went to church to see the minister, whom he had only met recently, and thanked him for taking the time to visit. He shook the minister's hand and told him how much comfort his presence had brought to a man lying in the hospital, fearful and in pain. The astonished minister told my friend's father that while he appreciated the gesture, he could not take the credit, for he had been unable to visit the hospital after the operation.

Based on the various accounts gathered here, we can conclude that guardian angels are nothing if not resourceful. They have many ways of getting our attention, from appearing in dreams or poking into thoughts to appearing as animals or lights. At times, they speak loudly and stop us in our tracks. On other occasions, they simply whisper "do that" or "yes!"

Many who know me, including family members, will be surprised by the stories I've shared. As most of the people I interviewed will agree, these experiences are deeply personal and defy explanation. On top of that, despite the polls that show the majority of people believe in guardian angels, it is still not acceptable in most social circles to talk about angels as if they are real. Perhaps the respondents hide behind the polls' anonymity, or just pretend to be skeptical when confronted by strong disbelievers. Let's face it—mainstream society still generally thinks that those who relate to the non-physical world are weird. A belief in spirits and angels usually gets stomped out of us by the time we're four or five years old, when our "imaginary friends" are no longer acceptable. To make matters worse, certain charlatans only increase society's skepticism by perpetrating lies in order to capitalize on people's desire to communicate with spirits.

Consequently, many people hold their experiences tightly to their chests and rarely share, which makes the contributions to this book all the more special. In a few instances, the narrators asked me to change their names to protect their privacy, and I did. I hope that a forum like this, which encourages the exchange of guardian angel experiences, will inspire readers and convince them that their own encounters are both real and more common than they might think. Many people will still declare with certainty that angels don't exist. But I've come to accept that strange things happen in this world, and such things simply cannot be explained to those who only believe in what they have seen.

Enjoy, and may the angels fill your heart to overflowing.

1
Life-saving Spirits

~

"It is in rugged crises, in unweariable endurance, and in aims which put sympathy out of question, that the angel is shown."

— Ralph Waldo Emerson

~

Divinely Driven Intervention

As I mentioned at the outset of this book, guardian angels occasionally intervene if someone's life is on the line while that person still has important tasks to finish on earth. This often occurs while driving, and Cheryl Caulder knows it all too well; her guardian road angels seem to be forever intervening on her behalf. Her life has been spared no less than three times from potentially fatal situations on the highway.

Her experiences, captured in Pauline Newman's *Heartbeat Angels*, began in the early 1970s. Cheryl planned to drive across Canada and looked forward to making it a solo journey. But her home had barely faded in the rearview mirror when weird messages began to form in her mind. "I smell death on the highway," registered in her brain. She drove on at first, ignoring the grim message. The phrase repeated itself, this time more vehemently. Finally, unable to block out the horrible words, Cheryl slowed her pace. "Just as I did, I rounded a corner and saw a three-vehicle pileup occurring right in front of me." By slowing down when she did, Cheryl narrowly missed being part of the carnage.

A few years later, Cheryl and a friend traveled to Radium, a little resort town in British Columbia famous for its therapeutic hot springs, outdoor activities and spectacular scenery. The pair took in the sights all day, then as the sun set, returned to their car to drive home to Edmonton, Alberta. Cheryl's friend took the wheel, and Cheryl claimed the passenger seat, ready to close her eyes and catch 40 winks. She had just settled into a cozy nap when she suddenly felt herself shaken vigorously. She awoke in time to find their car careening toward a mountain ledge. Her friend had nodded off at the wheel, exhausted from a day in the sun. With split-second reflexes, Cheryl grabbed the steering wheel and jerked it to keep the car from crashing.

The third intervention occurred in late fall on the highway from Edmonton to Calgary. The weather at that time of year is extremely unpredictable; foul, wintry conditions sweep in without warning, catching drivers by surprise. As Cheryl drove south, the rainy drizzle turned to fog and freezing rain. Black ice patched the road as the temperature dropped. About an hour outside of Calgary, visibility declined almost to zero. Cheryl could barely see the taillights of the vehicles in front of her. But traffic still buzzed along since it was Friday and people wanted to get home for the weekend. Cheryl had a sudden, overwhelming impulse to pray for her safety. She prayed out loud that she make it through these perilous conditions and home to her young child.

"Seconds later, a car roared past and pulled directly in front of me. I hit my brakes to avoid a collision." Her car spun on an icy patch and plunged into the ditch separating north-and southbound traffic. But it didn't stop there. The car continued on, out of control, onto the northbound highway. Cheryl believed her prayer had been in vain, and that she would surely die. But just as it seemed like she would crash into the rush of weekend traffic, "something took over the control of my car." Cheryl could only sit and watch in astonishment as her car somehow navigated itself across

Cheryl Caulder's life has been spared no less than three times on the highway.

four lanes of oncoming traffic and stopped in a ditch on the opposite side of the highway, without a scratch.

Afterward, Cheryl relived the moment many times and could not come up with any explanation for how she survived the accident. She concludes, "This virtually impossible feat instilled in me, even more deeply, a profound belief in Road Angels."

Life-saving Voice

In 1992, Tom Johnston took advantage of some good weather to work on his Pinto station wagon. He changed the engine, lifted the car up on ramps and climbed under it to adjust the transmission linkage. Somehow, while Tom lay under the vehicle between the two sets of wheels, his wrench slipped and the car fell out of gear. The driveway was on a bit of a hill and the Pinto started rolling.

Tom remembers, "My first instinct was to try to get out, but I clearly heard a voice yell at me like a drill sergeant to roll to the rear of the car. I reacted immediately and rolled myself toward the rear wheels. It seemed perfectly natural at the time. A moment later the car was on me and I was rolling down the driveway underneath it. I could hear my bones crunching."

The car finally stopped, still on the hill. Tom's body was holding all 2800 pounds of metal in place. His shoulders were touching in front of him so he couldn't breathe well. He tried to call for help but couldn't for lack of air.

Meanwhile, Tom's wife Debbie was sound asleep inside, having gone to bed quite late the night before. She says a voice roused her from a deep slumber. "I heard someone call, 'Help!' And then I heard another voice saying, 'There is someone calling you.' " She woke up and heard Tom's cry for help again. She ran outside and was stunned to see her husband pinned beneath his car. She blocked the wheel to prevent the car from moving any farther, then rushed back inside and called the ambulance and the fire department.

Alone under the car waiting for help to arrive, Tom heard the voice again telling him to lift. "My left arm was extended out past my head and I got my palm under the car and slowly wedged my elbow over on the ground until I had lifted the car enough to slide out. Understand, though, that my car had been lowered and there was only six inches from the frame to the ground."

Tom sustained a long list of injuries. He broke his jaw, right shoulder blade and collarbone and dislocated his left collarbone. His ribs also dislocated from the right side of his breastbone and crossed over on the outside of his ribs on the left. "That is how my shoulders could touch in front of me," Tom explains. He forgot the voice temporarily as he coped with the pain and shock of his accident.

When he returned home from the hospital three days later, the ramps were still there. Tom surveyed the scene of the accident, and observed something that scared him anew. He says, "I had been lying on a large slab of rock when I was working on the car. If I had tried to get out when the car started rolling I wouldn't have made it and I would have been crushed against the rock. There were scratches on the rock where my car bottomed out when it hit. By rolling to the back I made it off the rock and onto sand. The imprint of my body was still in the sand from when the weight hit me." Tom pauses, then says, "That voice saved my life that day."

More than a decade later, Tom still finds the events of that day hard to fathom and the feelings he experienced after realizing how close he came to death even harder to describe. "I don't know if I have a guardian angel," he says, "but I feel sure there's something looking out for me."

The White Dog

What would it take for you to believe in guardian angels? Some people believe readily, while others demand proof. I know several people who fall into the "if I can't see it, it's not real" category. Margie Begley says her father Earl was a member of this group until one night in the early 1930s. That was the night her father began to believe wholeheartedly in the existence of guardian angels.

Margie heard this story as a little girl. It happened before her parents were married. Her father had accompanied the woman who would become Margie's mother home from an early evening church service. Naturally, as part of the courting process, they sat out on the porch and whiled away the time talking. Before Earl knew it, the sun had set and it was already past 10 PM. He lived on a farm and had to get up very early. Since he still had a good mile and a half to walk home, Earl said good night and set off.

His route home followed the train tracks until they intersected the road to the farm. Earl had risen early that day, and had worked long, hard hours. About halfway home, he felt utterly exhausted. He lay down next to the tracks for a few minutes to rest, and promptly fell asleep.

The sound of footsteps crunching on gravel woke him some time later. In the darkness, Earl saw two hobos approaching. This was a very dangerous situation, Margie explains. "That year there was a depression and people would kill you for your shoes."

Frightened by the two men, Earl rose and walked quickly along the tracks toward his home. The men followed. Hearing them behind him, Earl broke into a run. The two men ran after him. Earl knew he couldn't outrun the bandits, and therefore decided that if he had to die, he'd die fighting. He stopped, picked up a stick and turned to face the men who charged after him.

Suddenly, a large white dog, "so bright you were almost blinded by his brightness," appeared out of nowhere. The dog growled at the two attackers, who turned on their heels and fled in the opposite direction. The dog ran after them, barking as it chased them away. Stunned by this sudden turn of events, Earl ran after the dog and called for it to come back. The dog gave up its pursuit of the hobos and returned to Earl's side. The strange, white animal walked the rest of the way home with Earl, but kept its distance. Only as they neared the farm did it come close enough for Earl to touch it. He reached down, petted the animal and found, to his surprise, that the dog felt extremely cold to the touch.

At the farm, Earl tied the dog up with a piece of rope because he knew his mother would be furious if he brought a stray animal into the house. He tied the rope carefully so as not to choke the dog, and then told it, "When I get up in the morning, I will get you the best breakfast a hero can get."

Earl went inside and upstairs, but as soon as he reached his bedroom, a mournful howl pierced the night. Earl hurried to the window in time to see the dog look up at him and vanish. Margie's father could not believe his eyes. He ran back downstairs and outside to where the dog had been tied up. The rope remained attached to the post, still tied in the careful knots, but the dog had disappeared. From that moment on, Earl Begley believed his life had been saved by a canine guardian angel.

Ouija Board Omen

Maggie's experience involves an omen that she feels her guardian angel may have sent her via a Ouija board. In her early teens, she and a friend were playing with a Ouija board, unaware of the risks. Most paranormal experts advise people who don't understand the spirit world to stay clear of the Ouija board because there is no way to control the spirits that may come through it.

During the girls' session with the board, they felt they did make contact with the other side. "Being a bit ignorant of the unknown," Maggie asked the board how old she would be when she died and how it would happen. To her astonishment, the board replied that she would die in a car accident at the age of 16.

She soon forgot the incident, but a couple of months after turning 16, Maggie's parents asked her if she wished to join them the next day to run errands. "I said yes, and that next morning I woke up to discover that my parents left without me," Maggie says. "I was annoyed." An hour after she awoke, Maggie's parents called from the hospital. They had been struck by a transport truck an hour before.

Maggie spoke with her mother and made sure they were all right, then asked why they left without her. "My mom replied that she and my dad had tried for half an hour to wake me up and then gave up."

When Maggie heard the details of the accident, the Ouija board warning came flooding back to her. Her father had been driving the car, with her mother in the passenger seat and her brother directly behind her. Maggie knew she would have been sitting in the backseat behind her dad. The transport truck struck the car on the driver's side, right where Maggie would have been sitting.

Perhaps the Ouija board message was not delivered by a guardian spirit, but came through as factual information from the spirit world. Could it be then, that despite the omen of a fatal accident, Maggie's guardian angel felt it could save her from harm by making sure she slept through the morning?

Skid Row Savior

How many times has a wrong turn in life created a potentially dangerous situation? Sometimes the hazards remain hidden until we've waded into the thick of them. Other times, the danger is obvious but the way out is not quite so clear, like in this story, originally printed in *Guideposts*, in 1982.

Euphie Eallonardo caught a bus to Los Angeles in search of work in the big city. She arrived before dawn with five hours to kill before her job interview. Too wired to rest, Euphie opted to burn off her energy with an exploratory walk through the maze of streets behind the bus terminal.

Euphie soon realized she had wandered into a very impoverished area of the city and no longer knew the way back. Just as she grasped this disconcerting fact, a car passed and its headlights illuminated three men lurking in the shadows nearby. They followed Euphie as she continued along the sidewalk. Her fear mounted; she knew they were not taking a brisk morning stroll for their health. Frightened, she prayed desperately for help.

Just when it seemed the bleak situation could not get any worse, Euphie saw another man walking toward her. Surrounded, she felt almost paralyzed with terror. It didn't dawn on her until later that though it was still dark, she could clearly make out the man's image. He wore a work shirt and jeans and carried a lunchbox. Euphie guessed he must be about 30 years old and over six feet tall. He looked extremely serious, but his face was "beautiful."

Desperate, she ran up to the stranger and told him she was lost and that three men followed her close by. She explained that she had taken a walk from the bus terminal and could no longer find her way back.

The stranger told her to stay with him, and he would ensure she returned to the depot safely. Euphie gratefully accompanied the man and remarked that she didn't know what might have happened had he not been in the area.

"I do," he replied.

They reached the bus station, and the stranger told Euphie she no longer had to fear any danger. She thanked him profusely. As he turned to leave, he said, "Good-bye, Euphie."

She was well into the bus terminal lobby before it hit her. The man had called her by name. How was that possible? She ran out onto the sidewalk to find her rescuer, but he had disappeared.

How did Euphie know that the man coming toward her did not represent as dangerous a threat as the trio behind her? He did not identify himself as a guardian angel and certainly had no wings to give it away. But somehow, the terrified woman recognized his potential to help. Maybe similar escorts are there to guide us all through life. Perhaps we must peer through the darkness and allow ourselves to recognize them.

Emergency Angel

As a psychiatric technician who works the night shift at a small psychiatric hospital in Colorado, Robyn has seen, felt and heard several "out of the ordinary" things. She felt compelled to share this incident because it transcended even those unusual experiences and fell into the mysterious realm of guardian angels. Thanks to Rowena at castleofspirits.com for allowing me to include this incredible story.

Robyn's patients include many people who, for various reasons, are considered to be a danger to themselves or to others. This particular story involves a man going through an intense alcohol detoxification. Robyn noticed the man's behavior had changed dramatically from the previous night and she was keeping a close eye on him. She notes, "He was talking to himself, yelling things like, 'A man is in my room!' and he appeared to be unable to use his urinal." To Robyn, it was clear that the patient's confusion was worsening, but because she had seen other patients struggle with detoxes before, she was not alarmed.

In the meantime, the other psychiatric technician and the nurse on Robyn's shift were busy trying to find a way to take the patient's blood sugar readings. When the nurse arrived at work that night, she found that the glucometer, the machine that reads blood sugar levels, was not working and that she had no blood sugar strips left. She called the main hospital for the strips, and insisted they be sent over by taxi. She requested this without a second thought, even though the strips could have been brought over in the morning by the hospital courier.

At the same time, the other technician, who had both a good understanding of machines and a very creative streak, fixed the glucometer with a paper clip. This allowed the battery to power the machine. They then tested the machine with the necessary solutions and, to their delight, it passed the test.

At about this time, Robyn went to the nurses' station to report the patient's increasingly bizarre behavior. The nurse told Robyn that they should check his blood sugar as the patient was, on top of everything else, diabetic. Low blood sugar often causes changes in mental status much like those that result from detoxing. While the nurse was explaining this to Robyn and the other technician, they heard three rapid, distinct knocks at the patient's door. "We all looked at the door," Robyn says. "Glass windows surround the door so that we may closely observe the patients that are the greatest risks." But none of them could see anyone through the glass. The other technician on duty laughed it off, saying, "Oh, it's just the ghost playing with us." Given the psychiatric hospital's history of strange happenings, he was prepared to ignore the knocking sound. But for some reason, Robyn believed the knocks were a warning.

She immediately opened the door and checked on the patient they had just been discussing. Agitated, the patient pointed to the corner of the room and exclaimed, "He's right there!"

Robyn followed the patient's gaze. To her surprise, a "fiery, bluish outline of a tall figure" hovered in the corner.

She hurried back out to the nurses' station and, without telling the nurse what she had seen, insisted they check the patient's blood sugar immediately. The nurse was already preparing to do so. The results of the test confirmed their suspicions: the patient's blood sugar levels were dangerously low. They called an ambulance to transport him to the city's main medical hospital.

While waiting for the ambulance, they attempted to make the patient drink sugar water to boost his blood sugar, as they had run out of juice. Initially he refused. "As I stood there," Robyn recounts, "I saw a hand gently place itself atop the patient's hand. It looked kind of like the bluish flame that you might see on a gas stove. All I saw was the hand. My heart was pounding frantically and I felt like I was in its way. I immediately stepped back." The patient's eyes widened at the sight of the translucent blue hand on his.

The other technician in the room did not see anything, but could tell from Robyn's expression that something was amiss. "What?" he asked. "What's wrong?" Robyn looked at the patient and said without thinking, "Your guardian angel is here. He wants you to drink that."

For the first time that night the patient seemed lucid. He laughed and drank the water. Not long after, the ambulance arrived and quickly transported the patient to the main hospital's emergency. The emergency doctor informed Robyn and her coworkers that with a blood sugar level as low as his, the patient could have easily slipped into a coma.

After the patient left, the three sat together in the nurses' station, silent and somber for a few minutes, replaying the night's events. They began to share their feelings and concluded that someone or something had been present to guide them through the experience. The nurse had paid immediate attention to the blood sugar testing equipment, the technician felt compelled to fix the machine and Robyn tuned into the patient's behavior and some very special cues. Instead of dismissing the man's agitation and confusion as a side effect of the detoxification process, they looked beyond the obvious to discover the truth.

"Who knows what might have happened if we hadn't?" Robyn says. "There's no doubt in my mind that we all had help from the other side."

The patient was stabilized and eventually recovered. It would be very interesting to hear his version of events, and whether he remembers seeing his guardian angel at a time when his life hung in the balance.

Near Drowning

Whether it stems from a hormone-driven impulse or a misguided need to fit in, teenagers are known for putting themselves in harm's way, often driven by dares from their peers. Eva Gratton was no exception. On a summer's day a few decades ago, she tempted fate and received an unexpected lift from her guardian angel.

She had gone out for a day of swimming in the river with a group of friends. The group split up when it reached a dam in the river. Eva's group walked up on the shallow side and the others walked up the deeper side where the water was at least 30 feet deep. The gang on the deeper side of the dam dared Eva to dive into the river. When she hesitated, they started up a chant: "Sissy, sissy!" Despite never having dived before, Eva summoned up the courage to launch herself into the water. But rather than skimming the surface like a seasoned diver, Eva plummeted to the bottom.

Suddenly, Eva found herself tangled in the logs and brush at the bottom of the water. She panicked and struggled to free herself. "Through my panic, I felt someone grab my two hands and point them upwards. I heard a male voice say, 'Leave them that way.'"

Eva lifted her hands as she was told, then panicked and began to flail about underwater. Once again, the male voice instructed her to raise her hands and keep them there; he would help her out. Eva felt her body rise to the surface of the river, and when her hands broke the water, her friends managed to grab her and pull her to safety. "Much to my

Unlike this seasoned diver, Eva plummeted to the bottom of the river.

horror, when I reached the top, gasping for breath, I found that a couple of my colleagues had already dived down to get me," Eva says. Fortunately, they emerged safely and no one was harmed.

But the incident scarred Eva. Despite being saved by her guardian angel, she says, "I could not bring myself to enjoy the water ever again and was afraid to swim underwater."

Cory's Guardian Angel

These days, doctors often seem overloaded with patients, and the age of medical house calls is rapidly becoming a subject of the "remember when?" variety. Do guardian angels make house calls to pick up the slack? That seems to be the case, at least in one instance.

At seven years old, Cory came down with a vicious case of bronchitis. His mother Pam worried as her son's breathing grew extremely labored, and the doctors debated whether to admit him into hospital for observation. In the meantime, Pam let Cory sleep in her bed at night in order to keep a close eye on him. It seems she wasn't the only one on watch duty. This unusual experience, first printed on castleofspirits.com, happened over several nights.

The first night that Cory slept next to her, Pam awoke to an overpowering smell of pipe smoke wafting through the room. Disturbed by the odor of vanilla-scented tobacco and concerned about its origin, Pam got out of bed to find the source. But as she moved away from the bed, the scent vanished. After a quick scout, she determined that there was no one in the house. She crawled back into bed and immediately smelled the pipe tobacco again. Having seen and heard spirits throughout her life, Pam shrugged it off and went back to sleep.

Pam awoke to an overpowering smell of pipe smoke wafting through the room.

Over the next several nights, while Cory continued to sleep with his mother and battle the bronchitis, the same scent of vanilla pipe tobacco awakened Pam. However, on the last night that it happened the odor was sickeningly strong. Pam says she awoke to see the smoke from the pipe. Alerted by the change in pattern, Pam looked quickly at her sick little boy and noticed that he was not breathing. Frightened, she shook him awake. To her relief, Cory inhaled deeply and said, "Mommy, I'm so cold."

Cory survived his bout with bronchitis and grew to be a very healthy child. Pam isn't sure who the unseen pipe-smoker might have been, but she believes it was a guardian angel sent to watch over her precious child at a time when her two eyes simply weren't enough.

Guardian Angel in Disguise

Would you know your guardian angel if you saw it? Dorothy Baughman didn't recognize hers at the time, but remembers it well upon reflection. She had heard stories of strange encounters with spirits, but never thought one would happen to her. When it did, her experience left her so shaken that she wrote about it to *Fate* magazine in November 2002.

As a child, Dorothy was told that every person has a guardian angel. Her father believed in the protective spirits and told his daughter that she could count on them, too. However, after her father's death, Dorothy married, moved on with life and gave little thought to guardian angels. Occasionally, the memory of her father's words would make her smile, as she thought of all the tight scrapes he survived.

Dorothy moved to Montgomery, Alabama, where her husband worked for the Air Force. She found employment as a telephone operator, but the job required her to work night shifts. Since they didn't have much money, Dorothy walked home alone at the end of her shift. The big city seemed even less welcoming during those late-night walks, but she couldn't think of any options. The company paid cab fare for employees who finished after 11 PM, but Dorothy's shift wrapped up at 10. To make matters worse, Dorothy was pregnant and had suffered from a few fainting spells, but their tight budget simply did not allow for many cab rides. If she felt well, she hoofed it.

One evening as she left, the security guard stopped her. He didn't want her to walk by herself because two other women working for the company had recently been sexually assaulted on their way home. Dorothy assured the guard that she didn't have far to go and that she would be careful.

The first part of her trip took her through a business district, and as she passed the empty storefronts she could hear the muffled sounds of city life over the click of her footsteps on pavement. Her walk then took her into "darker, lonelier territory." In the quiet residential neighborhood, all the houses were dark and everyone seemed to be asleep. Her uneasiness grew as she passed an abandoned parking lot. She pulled her hood tighter around her head. Then she heard something that made her heart pound: footsteps behind her. She quickened her pace, afraid to look. Fear threatened to overwhelm her. As she moved faster, the footsteps also sped up, moving closer. Dorothy could feel herself growing short of breath. They were moving uphill and she knew she wouldn't be able to keep up the brisk pace much longer.

Her mind raced. Was this just another person walking home late at night, or would she be the next victim of a rapist stalking women in the city? Suddenly a hand grasped her arm. She screamed; her unknown pursuer immediately apologized. "I didn't mean to scare you," said the stranger. Dorothy tried to look at the man's face, but couldn't make out his features in the dark. "It was just a face surrounded by a fur-collared jacket," she remembers. "There was no way to read his intentions from the deep-set eyes."

The man apologized again, and said he had no intention of frightening Dorothy but he wanted to make sure she was all right because it was dangerous for a young woman to be out walking alone late at night. He smiled and offered to walk her home. Before Dorothy could say anything, he headed in the direction of her apartment, with his hand still under her elbow. Dorothy began to panic again. The man seemed to know where she lived but she knew nothing of his intentions. Without any direction, he walked her right to her home, a big old house that had been converted into apartments. The stranger walked straight across the porch to her door. Unnerved, Dorothy fumbled with the key, dropping it as she tried to unlock the door. The man picked it up, unlocked the door and accompanied her inside.

"You know," he said, "the city is really not a safe place. It can be cruel, dangerous and unpleasant, especially at night." He then announced he would make sure the house was safe and marched toward the back door. When he came back, he told the astonished and speechless Dorothy that all her windows were secure and everything seemed fine. "Make yourself some coffee, and your husband will be home soon. Good night." And with that, he left before Dorothy could say anything. "I ran to the window to see him disappearing into the inky darkness," she says.

Dorothy never saw the man again. She looked for him for weeks, but to no avail. Her husband didn't know anyone who matched that description and neither did any of the neighbors. She wondered if the security guard had sent someone to make sure she got home safely, but he never mentioned it.

"Are there such things as guardian angels, as my dad believed?" Dorothy asks. "Do angels dress in fur-lined jackets? I had always thought of them as white, shiny beings with halos. And what was I being protected from? Was there someone near my apartment who ran when they saw him with me?"

More than 40 years later, Dorothy still doesn't know who walked her home that night. Or perhaps she does.

Fished from the Pond

Two-year-old Helen Porter lacked the language skills to communicate her distress when she fell into her grandparent's fish pond, so she used the tools that came instinctively. She screamed, loudly. That, of course, had the desired effect and brought her parents running to the backyard where the toddler stood, shivering and wet.

In a 1983 issue of *Guideposts*, Helen's father William recalls the terrifying moment when he heard his daughter's shrieks. He and his wife had been standing in front of his parents' house, preparing to leave. Helen had wandered off alone, and her absence had gone unnoticed. Until the screams, that is.

William remembers running to the backyard, heart in mouth, and seeing a very drenched Helen standing and crying on the stone sidewalk. His wife rushed to scoop up her daughter and comfort her. William suddenly realized there was something very wrong with the scene. His daughter stood at least 20 feet from the pool, but there were no tiny, wet footprints to mark her path from the water to her current spot. Even more curious was the fact that she wasn't still *in* the pond. He examined the pool and determined there was no way a little child could have climbed out by herself. Though small, at about six or seven feet in diameter, the pool held at least four feet of water. At that depth, the child could not have touched bottom.

Years passed, but the strange incident continued to plague the Porters, who kept up their search for a rational explanation for Helen's escape from the pond. Helen offered no help because she couldn't remember anything of the event. It did, however, leave her with a deep-rooted fear of water.

Helen finally sought the assistance of a counselor to overcome her hydrophobia. While living in Texas with her husband, a soldier, Helen met with the army chaplain who provided spiritual counseling and prayer sessions. He convinced Helen to do some memory regression work, which would take her back to the traumatic day she fell into the fish pond. Helen followed the mental pathways back to the moment when she knelt by the pond. She described what she saw and experienced, right up to the instant when she lost her balance and toppled into the water. Then, to the chaplain's surprise, she gasped and told him she now remembered someone pulling her out of the water.

"Who did?" asked her counselor.

"Someone in white," Helen replied. She distinctly recalled a man grasping her shoulders and hauling her to safety. The man promptly vanished once she was back on land.

The Porters finally had an explanation as to how their toddler survived a potentially fatal tumble. But that answer opened up a vault of other questions. Who was the white-garbed rescuer? A passing neighbor? Or was it Helen's personal guardian angel watching over her in her parents' absence?

Accident Prone

We all know people who seem to be, as my father aptly describes, accidents waiting to happen. They bump into objects, fall off objects, trip over objects. They also attract accidents; if anyone is going to be hit by the runaway grocery cart, it will be one of these accident-prone souls. Perhaps they serve as practice subjects for guardian angels, to teach the angels to stay alert and make sure nothing really bad happens. Nurse practitioner Nancie Barnett counts herself among those who are both accident prone and protected.

"Things could have been a lot worse in my life, but for the grace of these spirits I've managed to avoid grave injury," says the 41-year-old Californian. "They didn't reveal themselves to me or speak to me, but I knew that they were always there and it explained a lot."

Nancie first noticed spirits around her at age seven or eight. She used to see the deceased former owners of the house her parents bought, and often talked to them. Some of her relatives in Maryland lived in very old homes inhabited by spirits that she could also see. "I just thought every kid did this," she says.

Along the way, however, Nancie also felt a presence nearby that protected her. "I had many childhood accidents which could have been much worse. I had a bad skiing accident, but I felt someone there who kept me from really being hurt. I know they were there, because it wasn't a worse accident." By the time she was 10, Nancie felt sure she had a guardian angel.

At 16, Nancie received her first clear sign that a guardian spirit stood between her and harm. While out shopping, she inadvertently walked into a jewelry store in the middle of an armed robbery. One of the masked robbers grabbed Nancie as a hostage and held a gun to her head while the other thief ransacked the store. "The guy was fingering the trigger and the whole time I was scared but not really scared because I felt someone there to protect me from him. I was tingling all over, but I was really calm. I didn't flip out. Then they left and I had a meltdown." The woman who worked at the store told the police she couldn't believe how calm Nancie remained in the face of such danger. "Everyone thought I was in shock because I was tingling, but I knew that tingling came from the presence of whoever stayed to protect me."

Nancie says her accidents occurred more frequently after one of her friends learned to drive. "She drove recklessly and had a lot of accidents." Once, Nancie's friend rear-ended another car. Nancie wasn't wearing a seatbelt and her head hit the windshield, cracking the glass. But she felt someone holding her back from going through the glass. "I got that same tingling feeling and again I felt a presence," she says. "I didn't have that big of a head injury despite not wearing a seatbelt. Everyone said, 'You should have had a worse injury.' Even my dad said, 'You must have a guardian spirit.' "

Later, however, when Nancie tried to tell her father that a guardian spirit did in fact intervene, he laughed and told her it was her imagination.

Cars and Nancie made a dangerous mix. A second accident occurred while she sat in the passenger seat of

The force of the impact crushed the driver's side and pushed the Rabbit into a parked car, thus crushing the passenger side.

her friend Chris' VW Rabbit as they drove to college. A driver in a Volvo ran a stop sign and hit the Rabbit. The force of the impact crushed the driver's side and pushed the Rabbit into a parked car, thus crushing the passenger side. "The car was totally smooshed," says Nancie. The fire department had to pry the pair out of the car. Once again, Nancie had not worn a seatbelt and could have flown through the windshield, but for a second time she felt a guardian spirit had prevented her from being killed. "I was more injured in this accident, but it could have been worse. Everyone was surprised I walked out of it." Her friend Chris also walked away. Rescue workers could not believe they were coherent and able to walk. Nancie says, "I was tingling and shivering, yet I had this good, calming feeling so I knew that my guardian angel was there. I told the fire department workers that, and they immediately thought I had a head injury."

The accidents continued. Nancie joined a bicycle racing team while living in the San Fernando Valley. The riders trained at Balboa Park, doing their laps on the trails. Despite her history of accidents, Nancie rode without a helmet. "We were training one day and I don't remember much of it because this accident was bad. Some people suddenly moved in front of us, so I moved off the bike path, but I ended up falling and hitting my head."

That simple account belies the severity of the situation. Witnesses later told Nancie that in trying to maneuver out of an elderly couple's way she launched off her bike and landed hard on her head. Unconscious on the trail, Nancie suffered a seizure; the other cyclists placed an urgent call to paramedics. She regained consciousness in the hospital emergency room, woke up again during a CAT scan, and came to once more in the intensive care unit. "I knew it was bad, but I also knew it could have been worse and wasn't," says Nancie. "I felt my guardian angel with me."

Nancie somehow managed to stay coherent enough during her waking moments to give hospital staff her personal information. The hospital summoned her father and he arrived saying he couldn't believe she survived. "He said I must either have a guardian angel or a big fat rabbit's foot." Nancie had no memory of the accident or the events that followed for the next week. Doctors told her that she suffered acute swelling of the brain. They could not understand why she was not in a coma as most patients would be with similar injuries.

Nancie now wears seatbelts and helmets, aware that there is no point tempting fate. But she is more certain than ever that a guardian angel protects her. "I haven't ever seen anything, just felt tingly. It didn't choose to communicate and I didn't know who it was, but I always knew it would be back."

In October 2002, Nancie's father died in a Colorado hospital after a protracted battle with cancer. Nancie fell apart when she received the news, then recovered to attend the funeral and deliver her father's eulogy. Throughout the ordeal she noticed her face, particularly her cheeks, tingling. She had been very close to her father, and felt his presence support her, but it wasn't until after his burial that she asked a psychic about the ongoing tingling sensation. The psychic confirmed that her father's spirit stayed near Nancie and it was his comforting kisses that caused her face to tingle. "He was there the whole time from day one," Nancie says. "He never left me. And he has been watching over me since."

Recently, Nancie's accident-prone nature surfaced in a grocery store, where she slipped on some crushed olives and went down hard on the floor. "Everyone was surprised I didn't break my ankle, but he was with me." She is convinced that her father will be her permanent guardian spirit from now on. "He was a lawyer, a very traditional guy who thought I had an overactive imagination *and* was very lucky. It's funny," Nancie adds, "because now that my father is on the other side, he understands the spirits that he once did not believe in."

Comforted by the belief that spirits walk side by side with her down her life path, Nancie worries less about accidents and concentrates more on accepting the wonders of life that she can't understand.

Angel of Mercy

Born naturally intuitive and empathic, Mary Clark definitely feels protected by guardian angels. On more than one occasion, she says, her guardian spirits intervened and saved her life. She also claims that one very special Christmas, they not only prevented her death but called upon her to act as an earthbound angel while a young mother lay fatally injured in the street.

Mary lists many incidents to support her belief that the spirits protect her. In February 2001, she was driving home to Minneapolis, Minnesota from a trip to Southern California. "Before I left I had an upset stomach and a feeling that said, 'Don't go,' " she says. She chose to ignore the message and made the long drive, but after many hours on the road she fell asleep at the wheel. She recalls, "Something screamed at me to wake up just a second before clipping the corner of a tractor trailer." Mary did hit the vehicle but managed to get her car under control. "My Chevy was battered with $2500 in damage, but otherwise I was unhurt."

Months later, she was planning a trip to visit a friend in Ireland and her itinerary included a stopover in New York. "I had an inner voice that almost screamed, 'Don't go' and it was so insistent that I changed my plans and phoned my friend to say I would come the following month." She would have departed on September 9, and her plans included a visit to the top of the ill-fated World Trade Center towers. Afterward, she realized that her visit would have coincided with their destruction.

December rolled around with no inner messages to suggest an impending guardian spirit experience. Just before Christmas, Mary was at home in Minnesota, dining alone at a neighborhood restaurant because her husband was working late. After her solo meal, Mary walked home along the slippery winter streets. She stepped off the sidewalk and out into the street at an unlit crosswalk. "I was about three steps from the curb when I was physically pushed back onto the curb," she recalls. "I heard the screech of wheels and a horrible thunk. I turned around and saw that a woman had been struck by a car.

"For years people had complained about this crosswalk because there was no light. The streets had been icy and although this is a small suburb, people drive fast." The woman must have been walking just a few steps behind her. One look confirmed the gravity of the situation. The injured woman's head had connected with the car's windshield, cracking the glass. She lay unconscious on the road as her two young children, ages eight and ten, stood nearby, crying.

Mary's head spun. She realized that there had been no one else in the street to shove her to safety. "I felt the spirit there. I felt my guardian angel was with me," says Mary. But she also knew she had a role to play in the unfolding drama. "The spirits literally felt like they were a part of me…like they entered my body and said clearly to go and help this woman."

Mary ran back and held the fatally injured mother, comforting her as best she could. "I told her she wasn't alone." Mary held the woman as she waited for emergency workers to reach the scene. The woman died there in

I heard the screech of wheels and a horrible thunk. I turned around and saw that a woman had been struck by a car.

Mary's lap before the paramedics arrived. "What is interesting is that as I held her, the children saw a golden aura around me and wings come out of my back," says Mary. "This is what the children told the police when they were being interviewed. No one else saw this but the children."

The experience affected Mary deeply. "I think it means that I should just be kind and good and help people no matter what. I feel that messengers come to watch that I'm walking the straight and narrow."

A few spirits seem to be watching Mary these days. She and her husband moved to Texas in June 2002. Just three days after moving into her new home, Mary saw what she calls a "shadow spirit" out of the corner of her eye, "just floating along." She didn't sense that it meant any harm, only that it was watching her. When it caught her looking at it, the spirit disappeared into the wall. After several months, Mary realized that the spirit wanted to protect her. It did not, however, harbor the same fondness for her spouse. "My husband had been making a sandwich near the kitchen sink when the light bulb above the sink shattered, nearly hitting him. After we told the spirit in no uncertain terms that kind of behavior was unacceptable, it stopped." A psychic told Mary the spirit belongs to a man in his 40s who took his own life.

To this day, Mary recalls that night on the icy Minnesota street as a sacred moment in which she realized that she walks this earth protected by guardian angels, and that she herself has a part to play as a helping, healing presence on the planet.

The Memphis Angel

This story qualifies as one of the most unusual encounters in this book. In most of the other stories, a distinct boundary exists between the guardian spirit and the person encountering it. In this case, though, that line is blurred and the message only becomes clear after the danger has passed.

In Liane Varnam's third year at Vancouver's Emily Carr Institute of Art + Design, she decided to take part in the student exchange program. She ended up in Memphis, Tennessee. "It wasn't my first choice, but it turned out to be the most transforming destination. I learned under the best art instructor I had ever had, with the greatest and most supportive fellow students," Liane recalls.

Liane majored in painting. The painting department in Memphis is located on the third floor, surrounded by windows and balconies with fabulous views of Overton Park. "I used to say that going to the painting studio was like going to heaven," Liane says. "I felt safe in the studio, embraced by the surrounding park. The studio was all leaves and light and laughter, a heaven suspended among the trees. I could paint there every day until midnight." Liane decided to stay for the full school year. One evening that spring, she was happily painting in the studio. Then, in a flash, everything changed.

Liane was working late, painting alone in the deserted studio until nearly 11 PM. Taking advantage of her solitude, she cranked up her music. She had erected a canvas in the corner of the room, stapling it to the wall "to get that wonderful feeling of a hard, resistant surface." She danced, sang and painted.

Then, out of the corner of her right eye, she saw a movement behind some easels. "I could swear I saw a figure move stealthily around some art work, maneuvering to come around behind me." She did not panic, certain it was her boyfriend from Texas, who was supposed to be coming to pick her up. He loved practical jokes and trying to scare her, although he rarely succeeded. She caught the movement again, but now it was over her left shoulder. Liane continued to dance and paint but stopped singing. She decided to turn the tables and frighten her boyfriend instead of letting him jump out at her. "If I wanted to scare him good I would have to time my jumping around perfectly," Liane recalls. "For that I would need to hear and sense when he was really close. I leaned over and turned the music down. I waited until I could feel his presence right behind me, and with a whoop of triumph I jumped in the air, turned around, and said 'Boo!!' "

But no one was there. She realized her plan had failed, but something else very strange also occurred. "As I was turning and landing again on my feet, to face empty air instead of a scared boyfriend, I felt a shift," Liane says. "All of a sudden I had stepped out of time, and nothing felt right. The air felt too close, the paint fumes suffocating, my clothes seemed to hang on my body with no purpose, as if I no longer had any need for clothes, air, or any of my senses. I put my brush down, packed up my paints, turned off the music and sat on a chair."

Everything felt wrong, like sitting in liquid instead of air. Liane concentrated on opening and closing her mouth to breathe. She scanned the studio over and over again. She didn't want to move. She didn't even know if she could move. She just sat and waited.

By the time her boyfriend arrived five minutes later, she had an overwhelming feeling that everything was wrong. Her senses screamed. She told herself she was overreacting, that it was just a figment of fantasy, that everything was just fine! *Breathe, just breathe.* She hadn't seen anyone or anything. *Breathe again.*

But it wasn't "just fine." It was "funky." "Funky in the South means that something is off, not right. Like mold and rotten eggs. I knew it hadn't been a person in the studio with me," says Liane.

Liane immediately told her boyfriend what happened. He didn't seem to care or take Liane seriously. She persisted, trying to make sense of what she had seen and felt. The incident left her totally unnerved. She felt lost and confused. She didn't feel that the presence had been evil or had a malicious intent. "I had definitely felt and seen *something*. I just didn't know what."

Try as she might to put the incident behind her, that feeling of everything being "wrong" and "funky" persisted. Her boyfriend was in a strange mood himself. Their conversation escalated into an argument and when they arrived home Liane went straight to their room, packed a bag and announced she was leaving for her best friend Sarah's house. Forty-five minutes had passed since the incident at the painting studio. She arrived at Sarah's shortly after midnight.

Sarah lived in what is known in the South as a "Back House." It was a tiny three-room house behind the main house on the property. It sat at the far end of the lot between the owner's back courtyard and a lane. It was charming and messy and stood on the outskirts of an unsafe neighborhood. Sarah lived in a pocket of suburbia right beside a jungle of poverty. "Memphis was strange that way," explains Liane. "Neighborhoods could change from safe, beautiful, sprawling homes to dangerous, dirty, rundown ghettos at a crosswalk. There was no slow disintegration to lower income houses in Memphis. You just had to cross a street to be transported to the underbelly of the American dream."

Liane, meanwhile, was just happy to be with her friend. She talked about her problems with her boyfriend but did not mention what had happened at the studio. That "funky" feeling persisted.

Over the next few days a cluster of strange events occurred. Liane remembers, "I found myself doing and saying things I would normally not have. I could not shake this feeling of everything being wrong. I started to become more and more fearful. The only thing I knew was that I did not want to be alone."

That sense of needing to be around people grew into an obsession, and Liane repeated to friends at school that she did not want to be alone.

Liane's friend Anne suggested that a soak in a hot tub on the top of her 15-story apartment building might be exactly what Liane needed to settle her odd mood and feeling of unease. They took the elevator to the top of Anne's building. A cat hissed at them when they got off the elevator, and Anne commented that this cat was normally friendly. She didn't understand why it was up in this hallway since it lived on the third floor. When Liane bent down to pet the cat, it hissed again and ran away. They continued on to the hot tub, started up the jets and got in. Anne had just remarked on the lovely view when, as Liane says, "We felt the earth move like liquid. The water in the hot tub sloshed gently side to side. I looked at her and said, 'I think that was an earthquake.' We got up, ran down the stairs and out of the building."

Strange events continued to occur. Through it all, Liane kept saying and doing odd things. "Once I said to my friend Sarah, 'I better call my Mom and Dad before I die.' She laughed and said I was crazy. But I did call them."

On her third night at Sarah's house, the two women were making plans for the evening. Sarah wanted to return to school and work in the fiber department. Liane wasn't keen on returning to the painting studio. Sarah asked Liane what she wanted to do—stay at Sarah's place and relax or go with her to school. Liane replied yet again, "I just don't want to be alone."

Sarah walked over to the couch and pulled Liane up. "Then you won't be," she said.

Sarah prepared to leave. Liane got ready as well, but in addition to putting on her shoes she did some extremely unusual things. "I took the silver jewelry I had been making and hid it in Sarah's sock drawer. I took my camera and placed it under her bed. I moved my clothes and packed them into her closet. I hid my books. It was as if, subconsciously, I was trying to erase any trace of me being there."

The pair went to school. By midnight, Liane decided to return to Sarah's place even though Sarah was not quite ready to leave. Anne, who had been in the studio with them, offered to drive Liane home. She dropped her off in front of Sarah's house, waved and drove away. Liane made her way up the driveway and around back to Sarah's little house. It was absolutely quiet.

Liane walked up to the door and noticed with a start that it was open. "I froze. I felt time shift back again. I had forgotten what normal felt like. Adrenaline and my senses rushed through my body," Liane says.

With sudden clarity, Liane knew that the last three strange days were all leading up to this moment. "I had repeated over and over again to anyone who asked that 'I just do not want to be alone.' And I had listened to my voice. If I had stayed alone at her house that night, I would be dead. I felt that the moment I crossed her threshold and walked into her house."

Liane knew intuitively that the intruder was no longer there. He had come and gone like a breeze. The only thing disturbed was the blind he knocked onto her bed when he broke in through her window. Sarah's TV and stereo were still on their stand. No drawers had been pulled out, no closet doors opened. Burglary was not the motive for this break-in. Liane recounts, "I walked over to the phone and called Anne's home and left a message to please come back and get me. I hung up the phone, totally calm and back in my body. That feeling of being funky had gone."

"I had been warned," Liane concludes. "I knew that my death would have taken place if I had stayed there that evening." She closed Sarah's front door and went to wait at the main house for Anne to arrive.

Looking back, Liane knows the presence in the painting studio was a guardian angel. "I saw an angel in Memphis. I heard it speak through my own voice and it saved my life."

2

Visions and Voices

~

*"Do not believe me simply
because I have seen Heaven
& Hell, have discoursed
with angels…Believe me
because I tell you what your
consciousness and
intuitions will tell you if
you listen closely to
their voice."*

— Emanuel Swedenborg,
*Concerning Divine
Love and Wisdom*

~

Vision From Beyond

Kelly Kautman-Dyer has seen and sensed spirits of all kinds, including childhood guardian spirits and the ghost of her sister's boyfriend. None of these, however, prepared her for the extraordinary night ten years ago when angels visited her in bed.

"I'm sure I have a guardian angel," says Kelly. She concluded this after what she calls a very weird spiritual encounter. She now realizes her angelic vision didn't come without warning. But at the time, she didn't know what to make of the voices she heard when she went to bed. "It went on for about a week," she explains. "I would be in bed and hear voices. I thought I was cracking up."

Then the nightly voices escalated into out-of-body experiences. As Kelly lay down to sleep, she felt *something* take her out of her physical form and transport her to other places in her mind's eye. "It was moving really fast and would take me to a big, white house that looked very real. A business lady with an attaché would appear, walking toward the house, and then the vision would go away. I heard voices and had out-of-body sensations. It was too weird." Bedtime became a source of stress for Kelly. She would lie under the blankets next to her oblivious, sleeping husband, terrified that she was either losing her mind or that she was a victim of some strange, paranormal energy.

One night soon after, she saw the angel. She sensed a presence in the room and opened her eyes to see a white, chalky angel with wings hovering in the corner. But unlike her notion of what angels look like, this apparition was more like a floating statue. "Everything on it was fixed," Kelly says. "Its eyes were fixed. Nothing moved." She squeezed her eyes shut, very scared, and tried to convince herself it was a figment of her overwrought imagination. "I opened my eyes and it was still there." She tried telling herself it was the light in the room creating an illusion, and she fell into an uneasy sleep.

The next night, she witnessed the same vision. The motionless angel figure hovered silently in the corner. Again she shut her eyes, thinking it must be a result of the way lights shone into the room. Kelly peeked out from under the blanket, startled to see the figure now directly above her. "It scared the bejeezus out of me. I woke my husband up, and he just thought I was dreaming." Her husband rolled over and went back to sleep, leaving Kelly alone with the vision.

"The next thing I know, this voice in my head says to pray," she recalls. "In my head I said, 'I don't know how to pray. Just go away.' " The voice persisted; finally an emotionally distraught Kelly told the voice to pray for her. "Out of the blue, another voice started praying. It was beautiful. I had a sense of peace about me that I'd never felt in my life."

As the voice continued, Kelly had another out-of-body experience. This time, though, she did not travel far. She remembers feeling pulled backwards out of her body, then seeing herself lying in bed next to her husband. She traveled down the hall and through the front door then hung in mid-air by her son's basketball hoop. Not believing or understanding any of this, she watched as an exquisite, iridescent cloud rolled up. From within its glow, small white crosses emerged and encircled the house. "Three rows of crosses were put around my house," says Kelly. "I didn't understand the significance of any of it."

Then she returned to the house, to her bedroom and to her body. "It was excruciating. I didn't want to go back in at first, but after the whole experience, I felt this huge sense of peace."

Even in the light of day, the experience stayed with her. Despite her natural skepticism, she could not dismiss it as a dream. "I believe the angel was trying to warn me that I was slipping spiritually, so to speak." Growing up, religion was not a deep part of Kelly's life. "The voice told me to pray, but I had never done that." Kelly felt moved to include the church more regularly in her life. She also discovered a keen sense of empathy for others, and an inexplicable intuition about events that will affect other people's lives. "I get information to help people," says Kelly. "I am shown things, and then I tell others. It just blurts out. I don't know how I know it."

Kelly believes angels continue to watch her, and she is acutely aware of their presence. "They watch everybody, but some of us have a keen sense that they are there."

Attention-seeking Apparition

Assistance from guardian angels comes both directly and indirectly. Though many stories in this book recount clear, obvious guidance, not all messages from beyond are easily deciphered. Sometimes a guardian angel acts as a dramatic attention-getter to shake things up, startle us out of our normal routine and make us realize that we are not alone.

Take the incredible story of Don Navarro, which originally appeared on castleofspirits.com. Don can't remember exactly when he saw the angel in his home. "I really do not remember what month of the year that this was, but it happened in late summer," he says, "I was about 15 years old, so it was in the mid-80s." He lived with his mother and newborn sister in Denver, Colorado. It was bedtime, around 9:30 PM, and Don stood in the bathroom brushing his teeth.

When he finished his evening ablutions, he crossed the hall to his bedroom. Before he could turn on the light in his room, he noticed that the space already glowed with a bluish-white light. "I was puzzled because I had only white bulbs in all my lamps. My room had a somewhat elongated entryway, so at this point I could not see the source of the light," Don explains.

He walked all the way into his room without turning on any lights to investigate this strange light source. What he encountered stunned him. "To my far left stood a glowing figure," Don says. "It was not glowing like any ghost I had seen before. A pure, calming illumination radiated out from the very center of the figure." He sensed immediately that this apparition was female, although he could not make out any physical details. The luminescent woman looked "out of focus," almost hazy in the brilliant light. "I just stood in awe. She was so beautiful in her flowing robe. I know that I was meant to see her, yet she seemed very startled." Could it be that even guardian angels get caught off guard?

The angel's glow diminished considerably at the sight of Don, and she disappeared entirely from the waist up, leaving only her legs visible. She began to move toward him in what appeared to be a combination of running and floating. Don's heart leapt into his throat. He still stood blocking the entrance of his bedroom. The female figure exited his room through the doorway, and on her way out, put her hand on Don's left shoulder. Then her hand passed through his shoulder and she disappeared through the doorway. Don felt "slightly panicked, but mostly entranced and vitalized."

He turned to follow the shimmering woman's path and saw her moving briskly down the hall toward the living room. He ran after her into the living room, and by the time he arrived her full glow had returned. "I could see her very well, which demonstrated her energy. She was heading for the kitchen, where my mom was facing away from the doorway, washing a load of dishes in the sink." When he reached the kitchen doorway, he could no longer see the apparition. But there was no mistaking the bewilderment on his mother's face as she turned to face him, pan in one hand, dishcloth in the other.

Fueled by adrenaline, Don yelled, "Did you see that?!" to which his mother replied, "What *was* that?" When

Don realized he wasn't imagining things, his body filled with relief.

After they calmed down, Don realized he had called out to his mother from the living room; she turned from the sink, expecting to see her son, but instead saw the apparition. When he asked her where it went, his mother replied, "She just vanished."

"We were slightly shaken, but we could not contain our nervous laughter," recalls Don. At the time, he and his mother agreed that they had witnessed a mere apparition. In retrospect, Don gives more weight to the ethereal being's visit. "I like to think of her as an angel," he says. The sight of a guardian angel that night actually helped to ease some tensions in their home. "Some trouble had erupted between my mom and stepfather. I believe that the angel wanted me and my mom to feel watched over by her. She wanted our attention and got it."

Looking Skyward

For Myrtle Innes, growing up on the Alberta prairie in the 1930s and '40s meant a life with few friends and plenty of hard work. As a child she attended a small country school, where she forged important friendships with the tiny contingent of students. It was in this environment, isolated and austere, that Myrtle had her one and only encounter with angels.

"I'm 72 now and this happened when I was 10. It's as vivid today as it was at that time," she recalls cheerfully. "It was my first encounter with anything different and it wasn't until I was in my 40s that I discovered it wasn't normal."

In 1941, Myrtle attended Grade 5 at the one-room rural school. There were very few children in the school at the time, and one of them, a girl we'll call Laura for this story (at Myrtle's request), became one of Myrtle's closest friends. In the middle of the school year, Laura suddenly became very ill and was rushed to the local hospital where she died. "I was devastated," recalls Myrtle. "My world just fell apart because I had so few friends."

Myrtle's mother took her to Laura's funeral service and then to the small local cemetery to witness the burial. Myrtle still remembers watching in agony as her friend's casket was lowered into the ground. Amid the solemnity of the service, as all gathered focused their eyes on the coffin, she cast hers skyward.

"I don't know why I looked in the sky but I saw these two angels taking Laura to heaven. My Sunday school lessons taught me that Laura died and went to live with

God, and I definitely believed it. And standing there, I literally saw her go. These two ladies had long white gowns and bare feet. They hovered side by side with their arms outstretched, and Laura lay across their arms as they glided upward."

No one else at the funeral noticed the vision, and Myrtle was equally unaware that she was the only person who saw the two angels. "Behind them was a ladder, not the type I knew with rungs, but one made of flaxen hair. It was very fine and filmy. It floated behind them and rose, curled up at the bottom, as they rose. They just kept going and I watched as they ascended until they were just too tiny to see."

The experience bothered the young farm child. She was confused for a long time about their lack of wings, and she wondered about the purpose of the ladder and why the angels were human-sized but not translucent. "They were as vivid as anyone standing around the grave," says Myrtle. "They didn't fade away. Distance took them away."

Myrtle attended another funeral six or seven years later. Though it took place in the same cemetery, she saw no angels and assumed she must have missed that part of the ceremony. She attended more funerals throughout her life, but never saw any more angels. She wondered if perhaps she was missing a vital part of the service. Finally, at one service, she mentioned to an acquaintance that she thought it was a beautiful ceremony, but that she "missed the angels again."

"You saw what?" the astonished woman replied. Myrtle laughs in recollection. "She alerted me to the fact that this was not normal, and not something everything else saw."

Suddenly aware that her experience was unusual, Myrtle reflected on its meaning. She found many questions and few answers. The vision had been so vivid, so why wouldn't everyone else see it? Why then and never since? She concluded that the death of her friend was very traumatic for her young soul, and the vision was a gift to help her through the grief.

Wake-up Call

Even people who are tuned into angels often discover things they didn't know about the wisdom of the "Winged Ones." Former radio broadcaster Sandra Bell learned this during a late-night drive that almost proved to be her last. This story was chronicled in the book *Heartbeat Angels* by Pauline Newman.

If you ever drive through the prairies, either in Canada or the United States, you will experience an unrelenting expanse of flat, paved highway stretching to the horizon. You will even start to appreciate prairie jokes about watching your dog run away—for three days. Some people find themselves practically hypnotized by the yellow line on the highway, and at night the chore of driving shifts from tedious to treacherous. Sandra Bell experienced this firsthand as she made her way to Great Falls, Montana, one evening. A professional writer and lecturer, she made the long trip, part of a lecture series promoting her work on angels, alone. She aimed to arrive in time for a radio interview at 10 AM the next morning. But as the

Some people find themselves practically hypnotized by the highway, and at night driving shifts from tedious to treacherous.

hours dragged by she could feel her energy drain. The steering wheel became an object to lean on to stay upright as she sped down the interstate highway.

"I sang and slapped my face to stay awake," she recalls. Sandra also carried on little internal conversations with her angels, expressing her gratitude for their guidance. The angels had helped her find work that would allow others to learn more about themselves. This internal communication with her angels was nothing new; at the start of the tour Sandra had asked her guardian angels to help her avoid running over any animals while she drove.

On this night, Sandra's eyes slid shut as sleepiness overcame her. Suddenly, a male voice jolted her awake: "Sandra, wake up! You're going to hit an animal!" Responding instinctively, Sandra's foot jumped to the brake and jammed on it hard. When the car stopped, she saw the two gleaming eyes of a rabbit paralyzed with fear in the middle of the road. When the animal realized it was safe, it hopped away. Sandra, meanwhile, had an opportunity to take in her surroundings as well, and was stunned by what she saw. Even prairie roads have the odd hill, and she had been headed directly for a steep embankment at 60 miles per hour. Her car now sat mere inches from a flimsy guardrail, the only barrier between Sandra and the 55-foot drop.

Looking back, Sandra realized how wise her guardian angel had been to use the threat of hitting an animal to rouse her rather than alerting her to impending doom. "I probably would have freaked out and gone right over the edge." To this day, Sandra values the lesson the angels taught her that night: to look beyond the obvious and stay open to the many ways angels can protect and guide her.

James

Some theories suggest that children need several guardian angels because they are vulnerable and require protection. The notion follows that as children grow more aware of dangers around them, most, though not all, guardian angels leave. I have always believed that young children can see their angels because no one has yet told them such beings do not exist. Their eyes and spirits are open to seeing without judgment. Adults tend to trivialize these sightings as "imaginary friends," and speak with a cynical tone that eventually penetrates the children's psyches and may cause them to doubt what they see. But as one mother in Australia found out (and recounted on castleofspirits.com), children may even show you their angels if left alone with a box of crayons.

When Kylie's daughter was about 16 months, she began to talk to a "friend" called James. In fact, his name was one of the first words she uttered. At first, Kylie assumed her daughter referred to her cousin James. "But I realized one day that she started talking about this friend before she had heard of her cousin," Kylie says.

Kylie's daughter maintained her friendship with James, and spent hours chatting with him. Then, when she was three, she gave her mother a glimpse of the man who accompanies her everywhere.

While her daughter was drawing with a neighbor's child, Kylie heard James' name come up. About five minutes later the children appeared carrying large pieces of paper, and the toddler said that she had a present for

Kylie. "She gave me a picture of a smiling figure with two large circles behind it. She told me it was a picture of James. When I asked her what the circle things were, she said they were wings!"

Since then, Kylie has contemplated the thought that James is a guardian angel. She even tried to capture his spirit on film, but to no avail. She doesn't worry about his presence. "From the lovely picture she drew, it looks like he is a happy friend, and I know he has provided her with hours of company," says Kylie.

She recently noticed that her young son, now two years old, chatters with his own invisible friend. Kylie wonders if James has also made himself visible to her son. She is patiently waiting until his language evolves to ask him.

Out-of-body Instruction

Connecting with guardian angels does not require a formal ceremony or invocation, according to experts in the field. Author Doreen Virtue states that one can ask for angelic help simply by writing a letter spelling out the problem, calling the angels mentally for help or stating a question out loud. Meditation is another accepted method. An article by Robert Graham, entitled "Angel Talk: Are You Listening?" suggests we should focus on breathing and letting the body and mind relax, then "Communicate to your angel that you wish to connect to her/him. Wait in peace. Be aware of what happens. It may not seem like much at first. Be patient. Subtle changes will occur. You may see light, colors or form. You may be aware of a presence." One man discovered this path by accident, but it proved no less profound an experience.

In 1985, David Playfair took up meditation as a way to relax and explore a deeper spiritual life. He rejected formal instruction in favor of audio-cassette tapes he could listen to at home. "My experience took place prior to ever having any instruction, when I didn't know what I was doing," he wrote to me in an e-mail. "I used to lie on my bed and listen to subliminal message tapes. I found when I did that I would have a sense of hovering outside my body." David eventually discovered that he could lie on his bed and get the same out-of-body sensation without using the tapes. "I figured I was meditating," he concluded.

One night at about 9 PM he had been hovering outside his body for quite a while. He thought to himself, "You know, while I'm in this sort of trance-like state, and before getting up, perhaps there's a communication I could receive." The next think he knew, a dot of white light appeared. David finds what happened next difficult to explain. He could both see and sense the dot in his mind's eye. Within a fraction of a second the dot expanded to fill the space with formless radiance. "As it expanded, it was as if the light and my energy completely melded so the light became me and I became the light. That's when the communication came. It was huge and completely silent yet said to me wordlessly, 'We are pleased with your endeavors and all is well. Be happy and know that you are looked after.' " David felt a calm rejoicing emanate from the light, as it affirmed that he was moving in the right direction with his life. "I basically felt that things were as they should be and that if I had to put the message into words, I was on the right path."

For a moment, the light and message absorbed David, until his brain took over. "As soon as I became aware that this was happening, in other words, as soon as I stopped just being there in the moment, and thought about the fact that I was lying on my bed and this was an actual spiritual experience, I slammed back into my body."

The more he woke up, the more he panicked. David ran from the darkened room, turned on the bathroom light and began splashing cold water on his face. "I was excited and terrified at the same time." However, as he moved mentally and physically further away from the experience, it grew less terrifying and more comforting. "An hour later I was all aglow and it has stayed with me all these years. I have had absolutely no doubt about God and guardian spirits ever since," says David. "That was over 18 years ago."

That was the only direct message he received, but ever since he has noticed incidents that remind him that spirits guide him. "I've noticed patterns, like asking a question and the answer just being there," David explains. "I desperately needed $2000 to pay an unexpected university fee, and didn't have it at all. I kept asking, 'how will I pay for it?' Then I was in a car accident, and the damage appraisal to my car was $2000. I told the insurance company I would take the cheque and decided to live with the damage to my vehicle as it didn't affect the car's roadworthiness. So suddenly I had exactly the right amount of money needed to pay the fee. Things like that happen all the time."

Marie's Near Miss

Marie shared this brief but compelling story on an online discussion bulletin board in answer to a posting I placed in search of stories. She asked that I not use her full name, concerned with what people may think.

On a drizzly day ten years ago, Marie drove from her home down her street toward a major intersection. It was early evening; she had a monthly meeting to attend with a group of Therapeutic Touch practitioners. Though the rain made the streets a little slick, conditions were fair.

As she approached the intersection she thought she heard someone whisper softly, "Slow down." At first, she thought she was hearing things. "After all, I was alone in the car. I wondered 'what the heck was that?' and kept driving." She continued her approach, and heard a much louder voice shout, "Slow down!"

"It surprised me so much that I did just that," says Marie. "I applied my brakes even though I faced a green light. I tend to have a lead foot and normally would have bombed through it, but I was going very slowly." Just before Marie entered the intersection, she spotted a car out of the corner of her left eye. It came "out of what seemed like nowhere," racing through the intersection. The car ran the red light, missing her by inches.

The near miss scared Marie deeply. "If I had kept up my speed, I would have been killed, as the car would have hit me directly on my side." Of the mysterious voice, she says she couldn't tell if it was male or female, and she hasn't heard it since, but she points out that this was not just an intuitive flash inside her head. "This was actually heard out loud," she says. "It also made me start taking angels a little more seriously."

Indeed, after this incident, Marie explored the concept of angels, guardians and spirit guides more intensely. She recalls having many moments of what she calls "synchronicity." One night in particular, as she drove home from a pottery class and pondered the idea of angels, she began to feel doubtful, and wrote off the notion of spirits as just the sum of a vivid imagination and many coincidences. "I remember asking for a visual sign that angels were actually real and that I was not just making it all up," she says. "Seconds later I looked into the dusk sky and saw what looked exactly like an angel's wing."

Okay, she thought, interesting, but possibly just another coincidence. Then it occurred to her to ask for a more specific sign. "I said that if angels were real, I wanted to see an elephant to let me know that I was not crazy. Any kind of elephant: small, big, real, dead, a picture, whatever, but an elephant. I figured that I would need something out-of-the-ordinary to eliminate a coincidence, and there are not many elephants in Ontario!"

The next day, Marie visited a friend who had no idea about her little challenge for the angels. Marie had barely passed through the front door when her friend said, "Come and see what I just got." Marie turned to see what her friend was looking at. There, smiling up at her, was a little ceramic elephant.

As a result, she has a whole new appreciation for the voice that stopped her in time and prevented a possibly

As she approached the intersection she thought she heard someone whisper softly, "Slow down".

fatal accident. "Spirit guides, guardian angels, whatever…a big thank you."

Comfort for a Sick Child

It amazes me how traumatic events from very early child-hood lodge in our memories. Though most of my own flashbacks—thanks to sensible adult hindsight—recall fairly mundane moments, Gail Saivar of San Diego, California, carries with her a most outstanding childhood memory. In Leslie Rule's *Coast to Coast Ghosts*, Gail clearly recalls the night a protective spirit soothed her as she struggled with a virulent respiratory illness.

At the time, Gail lived in a large mid-19th century house in St. Paul, Minnesota. At five years old, she could not really understand why she felt so sick or why she had such difficulty breathing. Frightened and crying, she called to her mother from her bed. No response. Gail persisted, howling until her throat was raw, but her mother remained downstairs. She remembers wondering why her mother hadn't come, and she watched the hall from her bed for a familiar shadow moving up the stairs in answer to her calls.

All of a sudden, Gail saw a woman move from the stair-case, down the hall and into her room. The figure wore a long, white nightgown and had bright, green eyes. This was definitely *not* her mother. "Mommy?" Gail now made the call less as a cry for help and more as a query. The woman in the nightgown moved closer but didn't respond.

At first, Gail remembers being scared by this stranger in her room. Then something eased inside her, and she no longer feared the woman. At the same time, she felt her congestion and fever lift. Although the woman made no attempt to touch Gail physically, her presence seemed to bring about immediate healing. Gail recalls, "I felt better and was able to fall asleep."

The identity of the white-gowned spirit remains a mystery. Gail never figured out if the mysterious stranger was the spirit of a former resident of the house or a guardian spirit that visited her specifically, but she knows without a doubt that it came to help her. She continues to be grateful.

Strength from a Personal Spirit Guide

Just four years ago, Antonella says, her life qualified as a disaster. "I couldn't hold down a job or a relationship. I lived not knowing who I was." The Italian-born single mother felt stuck in a going-nowhere life in London, England, but the birth of her son triggered a series of events that would change all that. It all began with a trip home to stay with her parents in Turin, Italy. "That's when my mother finally revealed to me that I had a spirit guide," Antonella recalls.

To be fair, Antonella admits, her first knowledge of a personal spirit guide came during a 1992 visit to a psychic. The woman told her many accurate details of her life, her parents, her past and future. After more than an hour, as the psychic wrapped up her session, she added, "Oh, by the way, your spirit guide is a Native American

Indian." Antonella barely registered the information. "It went in one ear and out the other."

Other exceptional experiences suggested Antonella received spiritual guidance, but she didn't realize it until years later. On one occasion, she detected a strong presence standing by her side as she drummed up the courage to tell a former boyfriend that she didn't want anything more to do with him. "I felt someone encouraging me, saying 'Go ahead, you can do this, it's for the best,' even though I couldn't see or hear the spirit. But I knew someone was there for me." A similar sensation filled her once while she fought with her son's father. "I was thinking, 'Why am I going through this? Why do I have to suffer this?' And I heard a mental response saying everything would be okay." Rather than relate the incidents back to the psychic's revelation, Antonella assumed her mind was playing tricks on her. That's why she was shocked by her mother's news.

"After I had my son, I stayed with my parents for a few weeks," she told me during a telephone interview. "That's when my mom revealed that when I was three, she put me to bed and while I was sleeping peacefully she saw the image of a man sitting on my bed, watching me." Her mother possesses a deeply psychic nature, and therefore Antonella didn't doubt what she heard. The man appeared to be in his mid-40s, with darker skin and long dark hair. "My mother couldn't figure out his race; she thought he sort of looked Egyptian." The man stayed for several minutes to watch over the sleeping child before he disappeared. Antonella is convinced the presence that gave her strength and advice is the same spirit guide her mother identified.

Further confirmation came about two years later during a visit to another psychic in England. The medium knew nothing about Antonella, and immediately sensed the presence of her guardian spirit. The psychic said, "By the way, you have a spirit guide who is an American Indian," and claimed to see a tall man with white marks on his face. He added that this man had been Antonella's father in a previous life, a member of the Flathead tribe of western North America.

The information overwhelmed Antonella at first. "It's difficult to believe in a previous life. There's no proof. However, I've got three people telling me this person exists, so I have come to believe in him."

What kind of help does she receive from her guardian spirit? "If I'm in distress, sad or worried, that's when he will come to me. He will whisper to me, put his arm around me." The most recent visit occurred a few nights before the interview for this story. Stressed about her unemployment, Antonella panicked. "I'm looking for work now and there isn't a lot of work available in London. I was frightened. How will I pay my bills? How will I cover the mortgage? I have a son to care for. What will I do? I was unable to sleep, and then all of a sudden my spirit came to me, talking loudly in my ear as if to make sure I heard him, saying, 'Don't worry, everything will be okay.' " Antonella calmed down and managed to sleep. Two days later, she landed a lucrative job. "So he was right."

Though he has sent no warnings of danger or impending doom, her guardian spirit does seem to possess a sense of humor. While living in a small flat, Antonella discovered she shared the space with a small mouse. One evening as she lay on the sofa listening to music in her Walkman, she felt her guardian spirit approach her, take the earphone from her left ear and whisper, "You've got a little mouse behind you." She bolted upright, took off the headphones and saw, sure enough, a rodent sitting behind the couch, scratching at the material.

On New Year's Day 2002, her spirit guide enjoyed playing games with a bottle cap while she watched in openmouthed amazement. "I had made myself a coffee and left the milk bottle on the counter with the lid half on. I turned on the telly and there was an old American western playing, a classic Cowboys and Indians movie. Suddenly, out of the corner of my eye, I could see the milk cap moving by itself, twisting around on the bottle." She moved closer, within inches of the self-propelled cap, and all of a sudden it rose up and down in mid-air a few times. "I couldn't believe what I was seeing! I thought maybe it had something to do with the milk heating up, but the bottle was cold. It was truly weird."

More importantly, the 33-year-old says her spirit guide has taught her invaluable lessons. "I wouldn't be the person that I am now without him. I know I can't tell others because they would think I'm nuts, but he has helped me to know myself. My spirit guide told me, 'Whatever you think will become your reality in the end.' I value such deep wisdom."

Antonella believes that her awareness of her guardian spirit and her ability to hear his messages helped her get her life on track. "My life really started when I was 29," she says. "I came alive and discovered who I am and that I have a purpose. In four years, I've accomplished what I never did before: I now have a good job, I own a three-bedroom house, I have a healthy four-year-old son."

Do we all have spirit guides waiting to share some type of message with us? Perhaps, as Antonella suggests, it would be advisable to pay attention to the small details that may reveal a guardian spirit nearby, just waiting to be recognized.

3
Angels of the Past

～

"The Angels are…actually the leaders of men, their guides, preparing them, and there exists an intimate connection between what gradually develops in man and the task of these Angel Beings."

— Rudolph Steiner

～

Captain Joshua Slocum's Spirit Guide

Born in Nova Scotia, Canada, veteran sailor Captain Joshua Slocum is still known and revered today as the first man to single-handedly sail around the world. His solo circumnavigation in 1895, at the age of 51, places him at the helm of a small group of heroic sailors who have completed the journey. However, Captain Slocum's voyage on his tiny sloop (a single-masted ship) named *Spray* stands apart for another, even less known, reason. During his 46,000-mile passage, he became violently ill and, between the Azores and Gibraltar, found himself handing over the helm to the spirit of a pilot from the past.

Slocum details the strange leg of his adventure in Chapter IV of his book *Sailing Alone Around the World*, first published in 1900. It was July 26 and Slocum had been enjoying the fine food of the islands around the Azores. At the island of Pico, he luxuriated in a repast of fresh bread, butter, vegetables and many varieties of fruits, including plums. He also indulged in a white cheese supplied by an American consul-general before heading out to sea. Soon, however, the rugged captain suffered from severe stomach cramps. And to make matters worse, the weather turned nasty.

When the squall hit, Slocum felt too ill to take in his sails as he knew he should. Instead, he wrote, "I went below, and threw myself upon the cabin floor in great pain. How long I lay there, I could not tell for I became delirious."

When Slocum regained consciousness, he realized his sloop was plunging into a heavy sea. He roused himself to take command of his vessel, and was amazed to find a tall man standing at the ship's helm. An astonished Slocum noted, "His rigid hand, grasping the spokes of the wheel, held them as in a vice. His rig was that of a foreign sailor, and the large red cap he wore was cock-billed over his left ear, and all that was set off with shaggy black whiskers." Slocum assumed the man was a pirate, and wondered if he intended to cut Slocum's throat.

The man appeared to read Slocum's mind, and tipped his hat to the ill captain. "Señor, I have come to do you no harm," he assured Slocum with a faint smile. The strange man went on to say, as if his sudden appearance wasn't bizarre enough, that he was a member of Columbus' crew. "I am the pilot of the *Pinta* come to aid you. Lie quiet, señor captain, and I will guide your ship tonight. You have *calentura* but you will be all right by tomorrow." The man at the helm then added, "You did wrong to mix cheese with plums."

Slocum, still in agony, returned below the deck to recover from the effects of what may have been severe food poisoning. By morning, he awoke to find his pains had disappeared. Out on deck, to his astonishment, the mysterious man no longer controlled the helm but the *Spray* still held to Slocum's headings exactly as he had left her. "Columbus himself could not have held her more exactly on course," Slocum wrote. He also marveled that the sloop had covered 90 miles over a rough sea.

Slocum received a second visit from the Spanish sailor, only this time he came in a dream. The spirit told the captain he would like to accompany him on the voyage, "for the love of adventure alone." Once again, the man doffed his cap and disappeared, returning, Slocum assumed, to the phantom *Pinta*. Slocum awoke refreshed, with a strong feeling that the spirit was "a friend and seaman of vast experience." He could not attribute his entire experience to delusion or dreaming because that would not explain how his ship held her course "like a race horse" while he lay incapacitated on the floor of his cabin. He promptly threw all the remaining plums overboard.

In the fall of 1909, Captain Slocum left on a voyage to South America, heading for the Orinoco River and the headwaters of the Amazon. He was never heard from again. His epitaph reads: "...the *Spray* sailed on her last voyage, but she and her captain have joined the immortals and are sailing still..." Perhaps the good captain is now among the guiding spirits at sea who watch over that certain breed of sailor, navigator and adventurer—the kind who delights in taking on the many challenges and dangers of the open seas.

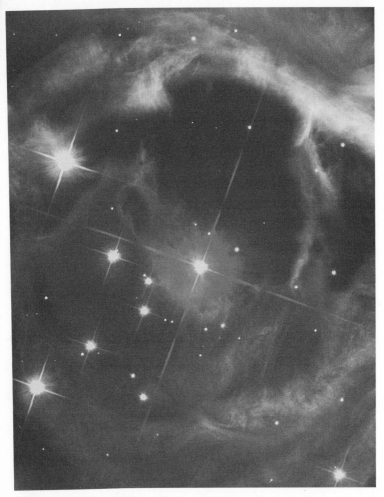

Are the lights that brighten the constellations more than the product of burning gases?

12 days later. This time, three other cosmonauts in the team, Svetlana Savitskaya, Igor Volk and Vladimir Dzhanibevok, who had just joined the others on the space station, also witnessed the sighting.

Angels in Outer Space

When looking out on the night sky, many people wo, if celestial beings make the stars their home. Are lights that brighten the constellations more than product of burning gases? We might simply relegate tl question to the ranks of dreamers and romantics, if weren't for a startling story that returned to earth with team of Russian space scientists. In 1985, on the 155tl day of its orbit around earth, the scientific team on board the Soyuz 7 space station witnessed an event beyond the realm of imagination.

The story, told by a Russian scientist who defected, appeared in newspapers in the 1980s. According to his story, three cosmonauts—Leonid Kizim, Vladimir Solevev and Oleg Artkov—were conducting some simple medical experiments when a bright orange light suddenly blinded them. Stunned by the impossible radiance, the scientists feared the worst—some sort of disaster onboard the station. Once they adjusted to the dazzling light, what they saw through the space station windows shocked them. Seven giant beings in human form stood before them, "in the classic depiction of angels." The figures towered at least 100 feet tall with misty halos and wings that rivaled those of a commercial jetliner. The scientists said the beings watched them for some time, smiling beatifically. They followed the space capsule for several minutes before vanishing.

It could have been considered a strange and wondrous one-time incident if the seven beings hadn't reappeared

"They were glowing," the crew reported. "We were truly overwhelmed. There was a great orange light and through it we could see the figures of seven angels. They were smiling as though they shared a glorious secret, but within a few minutes, they were gone, and we never saw them again." Just as mysteriously as they appeared, the group of seven disappeared.

Since this report surfaced, some people have speculated that the Hubble Space Telescope captured images of such ethereal beings, and that NASA, the Vatican, the European Space Agency and the French government possess "proof" that angels do indeed inhabit the heavens. I found several websites dedicated to the theory that the angelic beings have been spotted in the Southern Hemisphere, in a three billion-year-old cluster of stars called the Carina Constellation. The Carina star cluster, also called the Southern Pleiades, is known as one of the most beautiful and bright constellations, as it contains the second brightest star in the sky—*alpha Car*, or Canopus. Writers on these websites postulate that the Vatican squelched any release of the information because it believes these smiling figures are not really angels, but some other ominous beings that disguise themselves as beings of light. I have not been able to verify any of the conspiracy allegations.

Whatever the case, the astonishing experiences of the Russian space crew suggest there is much more to this universe than meets the earthbound eye.

George Washington's Vision of Angels

In the bleakest days of the American War of Independence (1775–83), George Washington received an angelic message at Valley Forge that strengthened his resolve and gave him a glimpse into the future. It took place in the winter of 1777, just as it seemed the American efforts to defeat the British would fail. Washington's army, greatly outnumbered, suffered several losses. Food was scarce, soldiers were poorly outfitted and many succumbed to exposure or disease. A growing number of Americans believed it was foolish to fight the strongest nation on earth and instead aided the British by providing them food and housing. Ambivalence and uncertainty about the struggle to break the chains of dominion gained ground. Nevertheless, General Washington remained determined to succeed.

This setting provides the backdrop for Washington's vision. One afternoon, after spending most of the day in his quarters, Washington emerged looking pale. He told one of his trusted staff, Anthony Sherman, that he had just seen an angel. He then made Sherman swear he would hold onto the secret until Washington died. Washington was already mocked for his habit of going into the bushes to pray before battle; this latest vision could send his troops running.

Washington explained how he had been preparing a report when he felt a presence in the room. To his

George Washington received an angelic message at Valley Forge, which strengthened his resolve and gave him a glimpse into the future.

astonishment, a stunningly beautiful woman stood before him. He asked her several times how she got in, for he had given strict orders not to be disturbed, but she refused to answer. Instead, she replied, "Son of the Republic, look and learn." The mysterious visitor pointed to a ball of heavy white mist that formed before her.

Within the mist, Washington saw "three great perils" destined to come upon the Republic. The first, a dark depiction of warfare between Europe and America, has been interpreted to represent the fight against the British for sovereignty. The second vision showed both scenes from Africa and a battle on American soil. An angel with the word "Union" traced on its golden crown placed a flag between the divided nation and uttered the words, "Remember, ye are brethren." Theorists have accepted this as a prediction of the slave trade and the resulting Civil War. The third scene showed a futuristic age of terrible battles in which America was nearly overcome by invading forces. Ultimately, the entire free world was united under a blue banner. This vision has been interpreted many ways, and most believe it is a prophecy yet to play out.

In conclusion, Washington told Sherman, "...the vision vanished, and I started from my seat and felt that I had seen a vision wherein had been shown the birth, progress and destiny of the United States." The angelic messages, on record at the Library of Congress, provided the future first president with the courage he needed to carry on the battle and defeat the British. It remains to be seen if his third vision will prove as accurate as the rest.

A Guiding White Light

One day in 1959, Elsa Schmidt-Falk ventured out into the Bavarian Alps for a hike by herself, not expecting anything more than a quiet time, a chance to enjoy the scenery and get some fresh air. The German officer's widow chose a path well-trodden by tourists. It wasn't a particularly challenging or dangerous hike, as long as one kept to the main route. Elsa, however, wandered a little farther than planned.

In a letter dated January 1959, she wrote of her situation, "Having started a little late for the return, and light beginning to fade, all of a sudden I found myself in a really dangerous position." Elsa had strayed from the safe path and would have to find her way back in the dark. She couldn't know that just one year later, a young girl lost in exactly the same spot would fall to her death.

As her fear mounted, Frau Schmidt-Falk discovered she no longer walked the path alone. "All of a sudden," she wrote, "I noticed a sort of big ball of light, and this condensed to the shape of a tall, rather Chinese-looking gentleman." Out there on the trail, this didn't strike Elsa as strange or impossible.

The mysterious man bowed in greeting and spoke with reassurance, then indicated that Elsa should follow him. He led her by way of a small path back to the tourists' route, then "disappeared as a ball of light."

Given the circumstances, some might assume Elsa's savior was a mere fear-induced hallucination. But Elsa seemed quite certain that the Asian gentleman was real

Elsa Schmidt-Falk ventured out into the Bavarian Alps for a hike by herself, expecting a quiet time and some fresh air.

and, more importantly, saved her life by guiding her to the correct path. What's more, the phenomenon she saw—a guardian spirit materializing out of light—has been reported by many other people.

Nobel laureate Dr. Charles Richet studied materializations during the early part of the 20th century. In one
report, he stated that skepticism guided his research.
"For my own part, having seen many materializations, I
can declare that I have never felt the very slightest awe.
My only preoccupation, and one that filled my whole
being, was always not to be duped."

But while conducting research at the Villa Carmen in
Algeria, Dr. Richet saw a fully organized form rise from
the floor. "At first it was only a white, opaque spot like a
handkerchief lying on the ground before the curtain,
then this handkerchief quickly assumed the form of a
human head level with the floor, and a few moments
later it rose up in a straight line and became a small man
enveloped in a kind of white burnous, who took two or
three halting steps in front of the curtain and then sank
to the floor and disappeared as if through a trapdoor.
But there was no trapdoor."

For Elsa, the guiding light needed no explanation. It
came to rescue her, and she trusted its knowledge of the
right path to take. She followed without question.

The Angels of Mons

Born of conflict, shrouded in mystery and enshrined in history is one of the most compelling tales of angels ever recorded. According to legend, the angels of Mons appeared on the Belgian battlefields during World War I to assist British and French soldiers in a miraculous retreat from the Germans. While historians have worked to debunk the tale as pure myth, soldiers from all three countries reported seeing angels and hearing those angels speak their native tongues. The story's veracity remains a genuine mystery.

The Battle of Mons occurred early in the war during the hot, stifling summer of 1914. The Germans advanced toward Paris under the Schleiffen Plan, designed to bring them an early victory by storming through France, outflanking the French and annihilating them, then moving on to Russia. The plan wrongly assumed that the British would remain neutral in the conflict. As it turned out, the Belgian mining town of Mons became the first point of conflict between the great armies of Britain and Germany.

The British Expeditionary Force (BEF) arrived in Mons in August to find the Belgian army in full retreat and the French completely overwhelmed. The small contingent of British fighters received orders to defend a position along a canal near Mons and hold back the seemingly unstoppable Germans for 24 hours. Two divisions of the BEF managed to halt the enemy in its tracks despite being outmanned three to one. Even so, the

British troops knew they would have to retreat in the face of such staggering numbers. From August 23 to 26, 1914, the small force of exhausted British soldiers carried out a fighting retreat, which took them to the French frontier at Le Cateau. They fought alongside the French to check the German advance before retreating across Belgium and France. Finally, the Allies halted the Germans and the Schleiffen Plan in the bloodbath at Marne.

Some time after the battle, soldiers reported seeing angels on the Mons battlefield, aiding the battered and outnumbered Allied Forces. British fighters saw a heavenly host of Agincourt bowmen led by St. George on a giant white horse. In the May 1915 newsletter of the All Saints Church in England, Reverend M. P. Gilson included the following account of the miraculous intervention, as told to him by a parishioner who knew one of the officers involved.

"They therefore turned round and faced the enemy, expecting nothing but instant death, when to their wonder they saw, between them and the enemy, a whole troop of angels. The German horses turned round, terrified, and regularly stampeded. The men tugged at their bridles, while the poor beasts tore away in every direction from our men."

What began as a trickle of reports soon became a flood of witness accounts. A British newspaper report stated that soldiers saw St. George as "a tall man with yellow hair in golden armor, on a white horse, holding his sword up, and his mouth open, crying 'Victory!' "

In August 1915, nurse Phyllis Campbell, who had worked at a field dressing station near the front line,

According to legend, the angels of Mons appeared on the Belgian battlefields during World War I to assist British and French soldiers.

came forward with stories of miracles and visions told to her by the wounded and dying. Upon her return from the war, she published some of the anecdotes in her own book, *Back of the Front,* which includes this passage about the retreat from Mons: "...as the immense wall of

the German army came up, a kind of luminous mist settled down between it and the Allied forces, and out of
the mist came two mounted figures—Joan of Arc and St.
Michael on white horses. The men who related these stories varied them in this way—that the British saw St.
George and the French [saw] St. Joan and St. Michael.
There did not seem to be any religious sentiment in the
stories, but those who told them had left the fight in the
certainty that victory was with the Allies." According to
Campbell, many of the wounded saw the angelic apparitions and were so convinced their salvation was a result
of divine intervention that they demanded medals of
Joan of Arc, St. Michael or St. George.

One of the most widely quoted stories came from a
wounded lance-corporal whose vision was published
anonymously in Britain's *Daily Mail* on August 12, 1915.
"I could see quite plainly in mid-air a strange light which
seemed to be quite distinctly outlined and was not a
reflection of the moon, nor were there any clouds in the
neighbourhood," he wrote. "The light became brighter
and I could see quite distinctly three shapes, one in the
centre having what looked like outspread wings, the
other two were not so large, but were quite plainly distinct from the centre one. They appeared to have a long
loose-hanging garment of a golden tint, and they were
above the German line facing us."

As the body of evidence grew, one man stood out as a
critical voice of the time. Arthur Machen dismissed the
stories as a total fantasy, and one he actually created.
Machen published a work of fiction entitled *The Bowmen*
in London's *Evening Standard* before the retreat from

Mons. The story depicted an outnumbered British Expeditionary Force miraculously saved from the Germans at a field near Mons by "a heavenly host of Agincourt Bowmen led by St. George, who confronted the Germans and sent them fleeing in terror." Machen tried in vain to convince the public that the reality of Mons and the fiction of his "phantom bowmen" had become intertwined to create a new myth of angels on the battlefield. He wrote: "I conjecture that the word "shining" is the link between my tale and the derivative from it...in the popular view shining and benevolent supernatural beings are angels and nothing else...and so, I believe, the Bowmen of my story have become the Angels of Mons."

Despite Machen's attempts to dissuade the popular view that angels saved the troops from certain death, the stories persisted and grew. The creation surpassed the creator. Many believers said that Machen had been inspired, either consciously or subconsciously, by some sort of divine connection to translate the soldiers' vision to a work of fiction. A year later, German prisoners of war corroborated the angel stories. They said they too had seen something similarly supernatural, and that just as they were about to overtake the enemy, the Germans found themselves unable to proceed. Their horses wheeled and ran in the other direction.

Kevin McClure's detailed attempt to gather all source materials in *Visions of Angels, Tales of Bowmen* provided even more currency for the notion that angels were present at Mons. His research revealed two separate sources for the stories: Bowmen tales that could be linked to

Machen's work of fiction, and angel accounts that preceded Machen's story. In the end, McClure concluded that whatever happened during the Germans' retreat from Mons remains a mystery to which there may never be a definitive solution.

Skeptics still dismiss the stories of angels as mass hysteria promulgated by a culture with an oral tradition of attributing combat success to divine intervention; similar stories can be found in the folklore and mythology of many nations, including Britain. The doubters hold that defeated men and overworked nurses created the notion of angels to explain the narrow escape at Mons. Others maintain that the angel myth served a useful military and sociological purpose during a long, drawn-out war. It kept the collective psyche of the Allied Forces and the citizens of Britain positive and stable. Belief in angels as warriors may have helped to carry the British through the horrific battles of Loos, the Somme and Passchendaele.

However, many people still believe that angels were present at Mons, where a band of severely outnumbered soldiers somehow managed a safe retreat against huge odds. That something extraordinary happened during those hot days of August in 1914 is not in question. Was it the handiwork of angels? As one researcher concluded, "I don't know if we'll ever know for sure."

4
Angels in the Family

～

"We trust, in plumed procession,
For such the angels go,
Rank after rank, with even feet
And uniforms of snow."

— Emily Dickinson

～

A Mother's Love

After her mother's death in 1999, Tammie became almost obsessed with learning about guardian spirits. "I was never into this until she passed away," says Tammie. "But I feel her with me and I would love to speak with her."

Tammie's mother, Betty, was just 63 when leukemia claimed her life. "She was my best friend," Tammie says. She believes the close bond she shared with her mother continues to this day, undiminished by death. Her sense that her mother's spirit remains with her began at the funeral service, when Tammie felt her mother's comforting hands on her shoulders, helping her through the event. Soon after her mother's burial, Tammie's dreams began.

"I had dreams of my father's death," recalls the Ohio native. "His legs were all black for some reason. My mother was there in the dreams, healthy and in her 30s, and we went through the whole funeral process together, like ordering flowers. Then she sat with me through the service and stood behind me while I greeted people who came to pay their respects to Dad." Tammie now realizes her mother's spirit helped prepare her for the not-too-distant future. At her mother's funeral, her dad Jim suddenly bent down to kiss Betty in her casket, and told her that he would see her in two months. At the time, the grieving daughter had reproached her father for talking like that, but he let Tammie know he had no fear of dying.

"My father had a lot of health problems and he went downhill quickly after Mom died," says Tammie. "I think maybe he hid how ill he was from us." Two months after the day of Betty's funeral, Jim fulfilled his promise to his wife. He died in hospital and Tammie discovered that his legs had turned black with gangrene as a result of his illness. While arranging the second funeral, Tammie asked her mother's spirit for some indication about whether she should arrange a military burial given her father's history as a soldier. Within days, Tammie found a box full of her father's service pins and medals. "I felt that was a sign that I should arrange for a military service."

Since then, Tammie says her mother's spirit continues to guide her with dreams and occasionally with subtle messages. A few years back, while going through a difficult marital separation, Tammie dreamed again that her mother was with her at a park. "There was a huge clock and I could see the giant hands moving. Mom opened a door and walked inside the clock, and I saw many clocks going around. All of a sudden she said to me, 'Time is wasting. Get your life together and be happy.' " Tammy woke with the knowledge her mother was trying to communicate. "I knew she was telling me it was time to make a decision about either getting divorced or staying in the marriage."

Tammie's children have also noticed their grandmother's spirit as an active presence in their lives. About one month after Betty's death, Tammie's daughter called out, "Mom, can you hear that?" from her room where she was practicing the clarinet. Her daughter resumed playing, then stopped again to ask if anyone could hear something unusual. Tammie investigated, and her 12-year-old told her that every time she started playing she could hear someone humming along. To Tammie's surprise, her nine-year-old son spoke up: "Oh, don't worry, it's just Grandma."

Most recently, Tammie encountered her mother's spirit while visiting her Camden, Ohio, gravesite just before Christmas 2003. "As soon as I pulled in to the graveyard, I got a strong whiff of her perfume. She wore Clinique's Happy, and I don't own it because it reminds me of her too much." Tammie dismissed the thought, and stayed to decorate her mother's tombstone and visit the graves of relatives buried nearby. As she worked, she talked out loud to her mother, filling her in on the latest news in the family, as if she was present and listening. "I distinctly felt someone watching me. I just felt her with me and I kept looking around, but no one was there."

Upon leaving the graveyard, Tammie's car radio began to play one of her mother's favorite Christmas songs. "She used to love to sing along to 'Grandma Got Run Over By a Reindeer' with her grandkids," explains Tammie. She started to sing along, recalling times when she and her mother sang together in the past. After that, two more of her mother's favorite songs played in sequence over the radio. Stunned, Tammie broke down crying. "I just missed her and I felt it was her way of wishing me Merry Christmas and thanking me for decorating her grave." When Tammie calmed down, she felt comforted by her mother's visit.

Now Tammie is on a quest to understand guardian spirits. "Before her death I sort of believed in guardian spirits. I felt my grandmother visit me once and sit on the end of my bed. And when my daughter was born in 1987, I saw my grandfather, who had recently passed away, standing over her crib in his old bib overalls." But her mother's death intensified her feeling of being watched over, and Tammie now reads everything she can find to help her understand the phenomenon. Tammie has even discovered that other spirits use her to communicate with the living.

"I had another odd dream involving a woman I work with," she says. "Her husband passed away, and about four months later I went over for a visit and discovered she was still deeply grieving." While at the woman's house, Tammie encouraged her to pull out pictures of the deceased husband and tell stories about him to help release some pent-up feelings. A few days later, Tammie received a startling message from the deceased.

"Her husband came to me in this dream. We were at an amusement park, walking down a path. He put his arm around me and said, 'You know my wife, you're a friend of hers.' I acknowledged that I was and the husband went on to tell me he had been trying to reach his wife through her dreams but had been unable to reach her. 'Will you tell her that I'm okay?' he asked. I said I would." Tammie's dream continued, and she encountered a young teenaged girl with red hair smoking unusually long cigarettes. The girl asked Tammie if she wanted one, and called the cigarettes "classics." Tammie awoke from the dream in a panic, but chose not to call her friend until she had a few days to think it through. She worried what her friend might think of her, but when she eventually told her colleague of the dream, the woman thanked her, telling her it came as welcome news and a huge relief. She also explained that the teenaged girl was her niece who died in one of the classic cars the girl's father collected.

Tammie hadn't shared her stories before because of people's negative reactions: "They look at me like I am crazy." But regardless of what others think, she feels grounded, safe and comforted by her mother's ongoing love and presence in her life.

Spiritual Support in San Francisco

Lying in bed one night in her Redwood City, California, home, Maureen wrestled with a personal crisis. Her life seemed strewn apart and chaotic. Nothing was unfolding as she hoped. "I was struggling," she recalls. As she battled her inner demons, she also felt a deep grief at the loss of her father, Dennis. His death from a sudden heart attack in 1993 shattered her spirit. She missed their talks and his wisdom. In her state of emotional disarray, Maureen felt the overwhelming need to share her confusion with her father.

"I just started talking to him," says Maureen. "I don't remember exactly what I said, just that things were hard and I didn't understand what was going on or why." She poured her heart's anguish out into the empty room and asked her father why her life had become so difficult. Suddenly, Maureen sensed that she was no longer alone. "I felt him in the room, and then I saw him floating above me." Her father's translucent vision smiled at her lovingly. "Then he hugged me," she recalls. "It was more a feeling—

he wasn't actually there physically. I got the sense that everything was going to be okay."

Maureen remembers that after her father's hug, a deep serenity imbued her spirit. "I was surrounded by a buffer of peace and calm." She likens the sensation to being wrapped in a soft, comforting blanket. "I'm a very tactile person and that is my primary mode of taking in information. When he held me, I felt calmer and knew that things were going to be okay."

After her father's spirit left, Maureen's anxiety also fled. "My mind had been racing with a hundred thoughts. Afterward, I still didn't know which way my life would go, but I felt that it was all right. I felt safe, no longer anxious, and I fell asleep."

A second incident convinced Maureen that her father's spirit still pays attention to the details of her mortal life. On the first Sunday in December 2001, Maureen celebrated the end of an extremely intense course in self-defense. "It was a life-changing course," she explains, "because we practiced real-life assaults where women are thrown to the ground and have to face off against attackers. It's pretty terrifying stuff for the most part." At the end of the course, participants invited supporters to watch them fight and celebrate their new skills. Maureen asked a close friend to attend, but she couldn't make it. "I didn't want just anyone to come, so I didn't have anyone there," she says. "Still, it felt lonely because everyone else was hugging someone and saying hello. I thought, 'This sucks not having anyone here to support me.' And then I saw my dad."

Dennis hovered at the back of the room, "like Mary Poppins," laughs Maureen. And he wasn't alone. This time he sat in a floating chair beside Maureen's maternal grandmother, both of her paternal grandparents and her uncle. "I was stunned. They were smiling; I could see them and feel them. They were really proud of me." As the other 15 women in the course presented their self-defense techniques, the spectators cheered along with the students. "So when I fought, my family was cheering me on," says Maureen.

Maureen reflected on the gathering of family spirits and developed a theory about her connection to that particular group. "What's interesting is that my paternal grandparents lived next door and died when I was four, but we were very close. I found my dad [after his heart attack] and did CPR on him until the paramedics arrived. I was one of the first family members there when my Uncle Neil passed way. And I was with my maternal grandmother when she was dying." Her family members were obviously touched by Maureen's presence in their lives, and wanted to reciprocate her kindness.

To this day, Maureen believes in both visions. "I did believe in guardian spirits before and I always felt like I could talk to my dad. I didn't question what I saw. I absolutely believe it." What's more, she knows that in some sense she still has a connection to her loved ones. "I haven't lost them. Their deaths are not mitigated exactly, but I feel they are still there and it brings me a lot of comfort."

After she decided to share her experiences for this book, Maureen also finally found the strength to share them with her mother for the first time.

Grandfather Knew Best

Patricia Anne Stewart's guardian spirit experience occurred over 50 years ago, but she still wonders about it. During her early childhood, a familiar voice spoke to her and saved her life, and it remains unforgettable to this day.

"I was probably four or five years old," explains Pat. "As a child, I endured many bouts of croup that would usually heal on their own." Croup is a common childhood infection of the respiratory tract that causes the windpipe and larynx to swell, and generates a harsh, barking cough. Pat's family lived on Toronto Island on Lake Ontario, just a ferry ride from the city but far enough to complicate medical emergencies. "When one was sick and in need of emergency care, it took a little longer than calling 911 does today," Pat recalls. "First, you dialed a long phone number, then the fire department arrived from its station on the island to provide oxygen and emergency care, as there were no paramedics back then. Finally, the Toronto Harbor Police arrived in their launch to take you across the Toronto Harbor, where an ambulance would be waiting to transport you to the Hospital for Sick Children."

One day, when Pat's infection flared up, her mother placed a pan of water with mentholated ointment on a hot plate in the bedroom to produce steam and ease Pat's breathing. Her family didn't have an automatic vaporizer yet. Pat's baby sister started to cry in the next room and her mother instructed Pat to not leave the bed or go near the hot plate under any circumstances while she was gone.

"While I was lying there, I remember it was becoming difficult to breathe," Pat says. "Then I heard someone say, 'Patsy, get up and get your Mom.' I remember the voice was male. It sounded like my maternal grandfather who had recently passed away and whom I loved very much."

Pat answered, "No, she told me to stay here. I'll get into trouble." A few seconds later, a little louder and with more urgency, the voice repeated, "Pat, go get your Mom. It's very important. Go right now."

Scared by the voice, Pat rose, went around the bed and promptly tripped on the hot plate's electrical cord, knocking the scalding water over her feet. She screamed in pain. Her mother ran into the room, surveyed the scene, and made the first phone call that would initiate the long journey to the hospital in all the above-mentioned emergency vehicles. On the way to the hospital, she asked in desperation why her daughter disobeyed her. "I told her, 'Grandpa told me to get you,' " recalls Pat. "She was not impressed at that point by my explanation."

However, when the doctors examined Pat, they immediately started giving her oxygen and setting up instruments to perform a tracheotomy. They informed Pat's surprised mother that the burns on the little girl's feet were not that serious and would heal, but she had a very severe inflammation of the trachea—not a normal bout of croup—and if they could not reduce the swelling, an emergency tracheotomy would need to be performed. The doctor said, "It's a good thing she burned her feet to get you into the emergency room. In about 10 more minutes, without quick and available medical intervention, she probably would have died."

Pat spent the next three weeks in an oxygen tent with lots of injections, tubes and bandaged feet. Fortunately, the tracheotomy wasn't necessary. "My mother told me some time afterwards, 'You know that person who told you to get up? Maybe it *was* Grandpa. He used to call you his angel. Now he was being yours!' "

That was the last time Pat heard voices, to date. But she will not forget the memory or write it off as the invention of a child's overactive imagination. "I would like to think it was my grandfather, as sometimes I sense the presence of my family members who have passed on over the years," says Pat. "Who knows? Divine intervention, my grandfather, or other angels? I am very thankful."

Snowball

Guardian angels reach people using myriad ways, from touching an individual's thoughts or intuition to appearing in dreams to relay messages. Most often, it seems guardian angels remain invisible, but now and then they do manifest in some form—not necessarily human—to do their work. Some guardian angels, such as the one in Sara's life, disguise themselves with fur and four paws.

Throughout Sara's life, she has attributed unexplainable incidents to the presence of supernatural spirits. The Florida teenager feels that she somehow attracts spirits because she witnessed many strange occurrences as she grew up. But the following event stands out as being very special.

When Sara was still very young, she acquired a small Lhasa Apso dog named Snowball. Raised by Sara from the time she was a puppy, the tiny creature accompanied her master everywhere. For 14 years, Sara says, she and Snowball remained inseparable. "I loved her dearly. She was always with me."

Snowball's age eventually caught up to her. She grew so ill that Sara took her to see a veterinarian. The vet told Sara there wasn't much he could do but he would try surgery to help the aging canine. "The veterinarian attempted to perform surgery on the old girl. I was devastated when I got a call saying my precious Snowball had passed away. I couldn't believe she was gone," Sara says.

Distraught and inconsolable, Sara cried herself to sleep that night. At around 2 AM, she awoke when she felt something jump on her bed. At first she thought she was dreaming, but she could distinctly make out the imprints of four little paws on the bedspread, walking toward her face. The curtains beside her bed swayed as if brushed by something. Soon, she sensed a dog lying beside her. "It leaned over and licked my face," remembers Sara. "I turned on the lights and to my shock found nothing there except some fur."

Still thinking she must be imagining things, Sara went back to sleep. "It wasn't until the next morning that I put two and two together. Things became quite clear and rather spooky. Snowball used to always jump up on my bed in the wee hours. She'd lay beside me and lick me before curling up next to me and falling asleep."

Sara shared her experience with her mother. To her surprise, her mother also had felt the dog's spirit sidle up alongside her in bed and snuggle. Sara draws this conclusion: "Snowball was a faithful dog to me when she was alive and even more so now. I truly believe she is my guardian angel."

It's interesting to note that the Lhasa Apso, a Tibetan breed, is known as a sentinel dog. Originally, its primary function was as a palace watchdog because of its keen senses and acute instincts for distinguishing friends from strangers.

A few months later, Sara received a new puppy named Bella for her birthday. One night, while home alone watching television with Bella asleep on her lap, Sara was distracted by a strange movement. She saw a white mist sprint across the floor. She convinced herself it was only her imagination until Bella bounded over to the spot where she had seen the apparition, barking and jumping at the air.

Now, Sara accepts Snowball's spirit presence without question. "Many times I've seen, felt, or heard Snowball, but I'm not afraid. She's only protecting me," says Sara.

Thanks to castleofspirits.com for graciously allowing me to incorporate this story in this collection.

A Spirited Family

Although certain belief systems suggest every person is born with a guardian angel to guide them through life, it seems some people are more adept than others at sensing their unseen companions. In one Alberta family I am privileged to know, it appears many members of the clan have a deep and ongoing connection to the spirits that guide and protect them.

Brenda Walsh saw so many apparitions as a child that she had to teach herself not to fear them. "Once I got over the fear, I learned to be more comfortable with my experiences." Only when she was much older did Brenda realize her friends did not share such experiences. Most of her extended family, including grandparents and cousins, had similar stories to tell, so she naturally thought *everyone* enjoyed the same spirit encounters. She was surprised to learn that the apparitions and sensations she always accepted as normal are still viewed by many as belonging to the realm of the supernatural. She believes that the supernatural is really quite natural. "It is not unusual for divine communication to come through," Brenda says.

To emphasize her point, Brenda shared several stories from her family's history for this collection of guardian angel encounters. I am extremely grateful to her and her family for their willingness to contribute their personal experiences. In some cases, names have been changed to protect the privacy of others.

The settlers of the Canadian prairies experienced harsh conditions throughout their pioneering days, especially during the lean years of the late 1920s and early 1930s, when drought and depression combined to drive all but the hardiest off their farms. During those years, Brenda Walsh's grandmother and grandfather were homesteaders in Saskatchewan. They lived in a tent with their newborn child while they waited for their new property, but winter arrived before they could move onto the land and build a home. To make matters worse, supplies grew short and restocking meant traveling several days to the nearest city.

"Grandfather made the long trip to the city to get supplies," Brenda explains. The trip demanded fortitude and good fortune as it was made by horse and buggy through the cold and snow. Meanwhile, her grandmother stayed in the tent with the baby, isolated and vulnerable on the prairie field. As the winter night howled and battered at the canvas, fear and despair overtook her. "She always prayed," says Brenda. "And she just kept praying that her husband would return safely and soon." Lightning and thunder shook the sky outside the tent. Suddenly, the makeshift home was filled with brilliant light, and an apparition of the Virgin Mary materialized before the frightened woman.

"My grandmother saw a full apparition," says Brenda. "The Virgin Mary told her that everything would be fine, that Grandpa would return soon and there was nothing to fear." Within days, a fully loaded wagon appeared on the horizon and Brenda's grandfather returned to his family.

Brenda's grandmother rarely spoke of her incredible experience. "She told very few people. My mother only remembers the story being told once to her as a young adult."

Brenda's grandmother maintained a connection to spirits throughout her life. In this next example of divine communication, her grandmother's helping spirit made a difference in the world of the deceased, although she herself was still very much alive. Could it be that we sometimes assist the guardian angels while we are here on earth?

When Brenda's mother, Liz, was 10 years old, she lived with her family in Pierce Lake, Saskatchewan. As in many small, northern communities, the residents all knew one another and shared each other's joys and sorrows. Brenda told me, "At that time, one of the neighbor's daughters drowned in a nearby lake. It was traumatic for the whole community." The 14-year-old girl, who I'll call Deanna, had been Liz's close friend and was quite attached to the whole family.

"After the funeral, my grandma kept dreaming of Deanna. She would see her in her dreams over and over," says Brenda. In the dreams, Deanna asked Brenda's grandmother to pray for her and help her. Her grandmother obliged and the dreams stopped. "Some time later, the girl returned in a dream to thank my grandmother for helping her to cross over and move on."

Brenda's father Bob received not one, but two significant encounters with guardian spirits to alert him to the hazards of driving with a lead foot. Bob's job on the oil rigs required him to travel all over the province of

Saskatchewan. Brenda says he tended to hurry from one region to the next.

On one particular day, Bob far exceeded the speed limit to reach his destination. "He was driving in southern Saskatchewan, on roads he wasn't familiar with," recalls Brenda. Suddenly, Bob felt a heavy hand on his shoulder. Surprised by the sensation, he immediately lifted his foot off the gas pedal and looked around over his shoulder to see who was behind him. There was no one sitting there. As Bob refocused on the road ahead, still perplexed by the sense that someone had grabbed his shoulder, he encountered an unexpected hairpin turn. "He realized that he could not have made the turn going as fast as he was before he felt the pressure," says his daughter.

Bob related the incident to his wife Liz when he returned to their home near Thorsby, Alberta, but he did not change his driving habits. On another occasion, Bob's work took him to Alberta's northern country bush roads to check cut lines. This incident still makes Brenda chuckle when she thinks of it.

Again, Bob drove through the area faster than the roads or speed limits permitted. At one point in the journey he glanced over at the passenger side of the car and realized another person sat beside him. "There was a man just sitting there," says Brenda. "It really scared him. He slowed down but the male stranger never looked over or said anything." Bob continued to drive and before long his taciturn companion disappeared. "He had a clear sense that it was just a hitchhiking spirit who tagged along for a ride, but that it was also there for a reason: to help him slow down. It shook him up quite a bit."

Bob also received guidance through an intuitive message too strong to ignore. This message saved his life.

Vagaries in Bob's oil-patch work meant he often didn't know when he would get called out to service a site. He had traveled into Edmonton, Alberta, to run some errands when the office called his cell phone with a message that some work needed to be done immediately in Edson, farther west. Bob was told to book a charter flight that would fly him out as soon as he could get ready. He made the arrangements and hurried home, but something bothered him deeply. He started to pace and told his wife, "I can't go. I have a really bad feeling about this." His feelings prompted him to pick up the phone and cancel the flight. The next day he learned that this very chartered plane crashed the previous night.

No one in Brenda's family doubted that Bob had been contacted by a guardian angel. "The message came through his body very clearly," Brenda said. "He was not just guided, but protected at the same time."

When she was in her late teens, Brenda moved out of her family home and into a place in the country with her boyfriend (now her husband). Growing up, she had witnessed several apparitions and was accustomed to seeing the spirits of those who had died. Now, however, she was about to receive her first one-on-one message from a guardian spirit. Unfortunately, she didn't realize the meaning of the message until it was almost too late.

It was a winter weekday. Her boyfriend had left for work and Brenda hurried to get ready to leave for her own job. "I had the uneasy feeling of being watched," she remembers. "It was spooky. I heard my name being called and I looked around the house but no one was there." She also noticed lights blinking and dimming in every room she walked in. "It was that kind of morning."

Without stopping to ponder who or what might be trying to get her attention, Brenda left for work. As she drove, she discovered that the previous night's rain had frozen into icy slicks across the pavement. "I was driving slowly, but at one point I started to slide and hit the ditch." The ditch turned out to be a 40-foot embankment, and she plummeted straight down. "I felt my life pass and everything slow down," says Brenda. When the vehicle lodged itself at the bottom of the ditch, Brenda sat in the car, stunned but unharmed.

Brenda reflected on the strange happenings at home that morning. "I was being spoken to and warned but I didn't pay attention and I feel I was really fortunate with that accident. I had to be winched out of the ditch, but I wasn't hurt and, other than a flat tire, there was no damage to the car. I certainly have someone watching over me." After that, Brenda began to trust the voices and messages she hears. She now lives each day believing that a guardian angel watches over her.

In the early 1990s, Brenda received a powerful experience similar to her grandmother's, only this message was meant for a much wider audience. "I was uneasy and couldn't sleep, and at 3 AM I finally got up with the feeling that something was trying to communicate," says Brenda. She had a bath, a tried and true method of relaxation, and while she lay soaking in the tub, she was visited by an angel.

"The room filled with light," Brenda recalls. "A woman appeared in blue and white robing. She was luminescent and I knew it was the Mother Mary." The next thing Brenda knew, the radiant angel before her was sending her telepathic messages. "It was a form of clairaudience. The message was very clear, though at first I wasn't sure if I might be making it up. I thought, 'Can this be happening?' "

Brenda grabbed some nearby paper and a pen, and wrote out several pages of the message she received. She says most of what she heard pertained to major universal changes on the planet. "They were messages of compassion. The main idea was that the world is in great need of change on every level, from the dishonor done to the earth to how we care for our children."

After the angel left, Brenda struggled for a long time with what had occurred. She told her mother of the experience, but was reluctant to share it with others because of its deeply personal nature. "It is difficult to talk about an apparition of a significant religious figure because we're not taught that we are of divine essence," explains Brenda. "We are taught that it is outside of us and not privy to common folk." She worried what people might think. However, she now considers the visit to be a blessing, proof that angels are always waiting, ready to offer help and support.

Out of Control in Oregon

Years ago, when Qulia Goodman lived in Oregon, she woke one morning with the feeling that something was wrong. She attributed it to concerns about her boyfriend, who would catch a flight out of Portland later that day. Qulia even went so far as to try to talk him out of going, but he had to leave and would not reconsider. Qulia drove him to the airport. "It was raining and foggy—nothing out of the ordinary there—when we left," says Qulia. "I watched with more than just a little trepidation as the flight took off. Then I headed home."

It was getting late and the weather had worsened, so Qulia decided to stop by her brother's work and wait for him so they could go home together. She says, "We left, with him in the lead and me following. We were doing all right until we came to a spot where the road slopes up an incline. That's where we hit the black ice." Despite their slow pace, Qulia watched as her brother's truck started to fishtail. She took her foot off the gas and slowed down even more, but her efforts to manage the situation proved futile. While her brother's pickup truck slipped, then regained control, Qulia's much heavier Dodge Ram Charger slid the second it hit the ice. She recalls tapping the brakes and trying to straighten it out, but it started to spin and was soon out of control. "The truck's tires hit the gravel at the side of the road and I felt it jolt. That's when I heard my daddy say, 'Cover your face!' I immediately let go of the steering wheel and threw both arms over my face."

The truck went off the road and rolled down a slope into a Christmas tree farm. It rolled two complete times, then landed on the driver's side. Qulia describes the horrible lurching: "If you've ever been in an accident like this, you know I was being bounced up and down hard in the seat. When it stopped rolling, I was very disoriented. But I knew that the engine was still running and I smelled gasoline. Somehow, I was able to reach up and switch off the engine without any problem."

Two men who had been following Qulia and witnessed her accident reached the truck and shouted to her from behind the vehicle to hurry and get out. Qulia guessed they also smelled the gasoline and thought the truck might explode. Later when she had time to process the accident, she thought it odd that she was able to turn off the engine, but couldn't find the latch to unfasten her seatbelt. She managed finally to get it undone and crawled out through the back.

The truck was totaled. The back hatch, ripped off completely, lay several yards uphill. Every window, including the skylight, was shattered except the windshield and the window on the driver's door. The running boards were ripped to shreds. The top of the rig was caved in except for the part directly over the front seat. Qulia's glasses were buried in mud outside. The truck had destroyed three rows of Christmas trees on its way down the slope.

Meanwhile, Qulia's mother had been taking care of Qulia's three children while her daughter drove to the airport. Qulia says, "About the time that the accident took place, she told my oldest daughter that something was wrong and posted her to look for us. She wasn't sure whether it was my brother or me, but she knew that something had happened."

At the accident scene, Qulia's brother carried her into his truck and they drove on to her mother's farm. The daughter standing watch reported to her grandmother that a truck approached, and when they pulled up, Qulia's mother already stood in the driveway, somehow sensing that one of her children had been through a terrible experience.

Inside the house, Qulia undressed and her mother helped her into a bath. "It took several washes to get all of the glass out of my hair, and my clothes were filled with shattered glass. I was wearing a new leather jacket and the sleeves were badly cut," Qulia says with some awe. "All that flying glass and not one scratch, not one drop of blood." Her right shoulder was slightly dislocated, but none of her injuries were serious enough to warrant a trip to the doctor. She didn't even have any bruises, although she did feel terribly sore and couldn't sleep while the awful sound of crunching, twisting metal echoed in her head.

So, what makes this story remarkable? "It happened in January 1991," says Qulia. "My daddy died in July 1988. I truly believe that he was there with me, telling me to cover my face so I would not get cut, and protecting me from harm. I don't think there are words to explain how it truly felt. All I can say is that I could feel him there with me and never had any fear at all."

Qulia still wears the ripped and torn leather jacket, her "lucky jacket," as a reminder of the day her father stepped in as her guardian spirit and saved her life.

A Father-in-law's Guidance

Many people, including several contributors to this collection, feel the spirit of a parent watching over them as they deal with the promise and peril of daily life. But Crystal and Jeff Conner of Tampa Bay, Florida, have an unusual connection to Jeff's deceased father. His spirit acts mainly as a guide to Crystal even though he died before the couple met and never knew her.

Fred Heinz Conner passed away December 19, 1986 after a long but secretive battle with leukemia. Jeff told me in an interview that his father and mother Rosalie hid the illness for five years because they didn't want Jeff to worry. As a paramedic, Jeff found out about his father's condition when another team on his unit delivered his dad to hospital. Jeff rushed to his father's bedside and saw how close his father was to death. "He was a fighter and he struggled with his last breaths," recalls Jeff, emotion in his voice. "I told him it was okay to let go and within 30 seconds he started going."

Flash forward several years to 1997, when Jeff met Crystal through a dating service. The pair bonded almost immediately and married in 1998. To this day Jeff feels there was something predestined about their meeting. Soon after they moved in together, Crystal felt Fred's spirit nearby. "I sense that he is always around," she says. "I remember one night I told Jeff that I smelled a very intense scent and recognized it as Blue Velvet cologne. I asked him if he was wearing it. He said no, but that his dad always wore it."

Crystal says she is often overcome by strong feelings, such as a sense that Jeff's father wants to assure his son. "I think it's a protective spirit," explains Crystal. "We lived paycheck to paycheck and always faced some kind of major decision. Jeff would say things about his father being disappointed in him, but I don't think he is and I feel Fred's spirit wants to assure Jeff that he's wrong." Crystal felt Fred Conner's presence acutely when she and Jeff struggled with a decision to move from South Carolina to their current home in Florida. "The decision to move was hard but now we're better off. I feel his spirit has been following us around and guiding us."

As evidence of his ongoing presence, Fred's photograph refuses to stay up on the wall. "I hang it up and it falls down," sighs Crystal. Even when she tried using the backing to stand it up, the photo still fell down.

Jeff and Crystal occasionally spot a bright light around the door to their daughter's room. Though it appears as if they left a light on in the room, the light always disappears when they investigate.

A conversation with renowned psychic Sylvia Browne confirmed the Conners' suspicions. In 2000, Crystal was watching Ms. Browne on a popular afternoon talk show and felt compelled to call in, knowing her odds of getting through were slim. However, to her surprise, Crystal ended up speaking directly with the highly publicized medium. Without being given any background information, Sylvia told Crystal that Jeff's father had been chosen as Crystal's spirit guide before his death, and his spirit now inhabits their daughter Katie's room. Crystal says, "She also came out and said, 'That's why the picture keeps falling down.' I hadn't told her about that at all."

To top it all off, Sylvia informed Crystal of Jeff's last words to his father, which Jeff had never shared with his wife. Later that night, Crystal asked Jeff if he had given his father permission to go. She repeated the words Sylvia had told her and stunned her husband into silence.

The news did not come as a big surprise to Rosalie, Jeff's mother. She often feels her husband's presence and is certain he saved her life a few years back. She had been cleaning a second-floor window and somehow lost her balance, falling through the plate glass to the ground some 20 feet below. As she fell, Rosalie felt hands supporting her. "It wasn't like feeling actual hands, more like angel hands," she explains. To her astonishment, she landed uninjured, and without any severe cuts. Even the hand that went through the window did not need any stitches. Since then, Rosalie likes to think her husband's spirit is with her. "But I don't like to think about it too much because it makes me sad," she says.

Jeff discovered his father communicates with his mother through dreams after his mother confronted him on two occasions about things she had no way of knowing. "I had purchased a dalmation because I was a firefighter, and I spent $450 on it, but when my mom asked me how much the dog cost, I fudged the answer because I had spent so much. The next night, my dad came to her in a dream and told her where I got the dog and how much I had paid. She called me and asked if it was true, and I had to tell her the truth," confessed Jeff.

In a second incident, he and a buddy went out drinking and ended up in a near-fatal accident in Jeff's truck. According to Jeff, the pair "should have been killed." Embarrassed by the circumstances, he made up another story to explain his damaged vehicle to his mother. However, Rosalie confronted her son a few days later, saying she dreamed of Fred and he told her what really happened. "It was bizarre," sighs Jeff. "She knew who I'd been with and what we'd been doing."

The Conners do not doubt that Fred's strong, invisible arms and comforting presence continue to help out in times of need. "Honey, I can promise you my dad watches over us all the time," Jeff declares with certainty.

Bruno's Voice

World famous baritone Tito Gobbi, one of the 20th century's most charismatic opera singers, recorded a special spiritual experience in his memoirs, entitled *My Life*. He prefaced his guardian spirit story by noting, "Though some people shrink from admitting it, most of us have had at least one experience in our lives which is totally inexplicable by what are called rational means."

To set the stage, Tito explains how he and his brother Bruno had been exceptionally close growing up, and as young adults they looked forward to sharing life's joys together. Tito became engaged to his beloved Tilde and Bruno, an airline commander, met the woman of his dreams not long after. However, on the way to his own wedding in Malaga, Spain, Bruno's plane crashed in sight of the airfield where his fiancée awaited; all on board perished. Bruno's wedding day became instead a day of mourning.

Many years later, Tito had earned both a reputation as an opera star and the income to fulfill his taste in fast cars. One day, he drove through Italy's notoriously narrow mountain roads at speeds generally reserved for professional race car drivers. He motored up a steep grade with a cliff on one side and a sheer drop on the other. As he approached a sharp corner, he suddenly heard Bruno's voice say: "Stop—instantly!" so clearly that Tito thought his brother must be sitting beside him. Without hesitation, Tito obeyed his brother's command and pulled over on a wide piece of grass. Seconds later, an out-of-control

Tito drove through Italy's notoriously narrow mountain roads at speeds generally reserved for professional race car drivers.

truck careened around the corner and jammed itself up against the cliff wall.

Tito ran over to see if the driver was all right and find out what had happened. The terrified driver told him that the truck's brakes had failed and he had only a few moments to stop the truck or it would have meant certain death for him. Panting and exhausted, the man asked Tito if he would drive to the nearest service station and send someone back to help.

Tito got back in his car. As he was about to set off, the full impact of what had happened rocked him. "If I had not been stopped at that vital moment, I would have been swept to my death as I met that lorry on the corner," Tito says. He realized his brother's warning saved his life. He felt certain his brother had been with him at that moment in the car, and it took him some time to convince himself that he had been alone.

Tito sat in his car, stunned. He says, "In those few minutes, the reality of Bruno's speaking to me was more intense than the reality that he had been dead several years." He trembled with the knowledge that he had not only narrowly evaded death, but also experienced something truly extraordinary. Tito got out of his car and leaned against the rocky cliff to prevent himself from collapsing. This time, the truck driver came over to be sure the obviously agitated Tito was all right.

Eventually, the nervous energy passed and Tito drove on to get assistance. But he never forgot the experience. "I *knew* that Bruno had spoken to me and saved my life. I know it to this day, and it comforts me."

A Voice in the Night

This story came to me through a friend of a friend. Rai Fisher's story, like several others in this book, acknowledges the deep, abiding love of a parent and provides comforting evidence that the parent-child connection does not end abruptly with death. Instead, it seems that parental spirits work here on earth, consoling us with loving hugs, bringing us important news and watching out for our welfare.

"I hope I can remember it all. My father died 20 years ago." With that, Rai launches into her story.

She describes her father as an extremely intelligent man who did not suffer fools gladly, but possessed a warm emotional side reserved mainly for his children. "His children could do no wrong," Rai told me. "My brother and I idolized my father." Rai's father also stands out in her memory as a very funny man who shared his sense of humor only with his family. He was far too dignified to make a fool of himself in public.

Rai and her family watched their father die for a year. He underwent massive heart surgery—a triple bypass and an aortic resection—designed to save his life. It may have succeeded if the invasive procedures had not set off a cancerous tumor that had lain dormant for three decades. Specialists determined the tumor developed from years of work-related exposure to asbestos. The date of the cancerous growth's conception no longer mattered. The doctor gave Rai's father six months to live.

"Ha, he was much stronger than that," declares Rai. "He lasted for exactly one year and three days after his heart surgery, gradually shrinking away from the burly, 200-pound man he'd been to a shadow of about 120 pounds." For Rai, watching the transformation was horrific. "He was such a fighter and was terrified of leaving us. But we were much more terrified of losing him. It was torture watching him fight to wake up and make it through every day." Rai's father died December 16, 1983. "It's the worst thing that's ever happened to me," she says.

The family stayed in Hamilton, Ontario, with Rai's mother for two weeks to comfort her and help with the funeral. Then Rai returned to her bachelor apartment in Toronto. Alone in the cramped space, the full weight of her grief threatened to flatten her. "For the first two or three nights, as soon as I put the light out, the demons would come and I would end up crying myself to sleep, or I'd sit bolt upright in bed, turn the lights on again and be in agony until I was too exhausted to stay awake any longer." Pain wrung her out and made her barely able to function.

One night, Rai sat in the dark, weeping inconsolably in bed. She stopped suddenly when she heard her father speak to her. "I was not asleep! I was not dreaming," she insists. "This is what he said to me: 'It's all right, love. Stop crying, I'm okay.' " Rai asked him where he was. Though her memory of his reply is blurry, she recalls he said something about it being "lovely." He went on to say, "I had to go, love. I was exhausted and I couldn't go on any longer." Rai managed to ask him if he was all right, to which her father replied he was doing well.

She intended to continue asking questions, but suddenly another unrecognizable voice spoke up. "That's all now," it said.

"No, I want to ask him some more questions," Rai protested.

But the voice remained adamant. "No, that's all now."

The visit, though brief, released Rai from the grip of her unrelenting grief. After hearing her father's words, she slept normally every night from then on.

While sharing this story, Rai admitted she still misses her father and can easily find tears within herself to shed for him. Even searching her memory to retell her encounter with her father's guardian spirit churned up emotions that had lain dormant for years. However, a bright side emerged. Rai says she's been going through a stressful time lately, and such times always bring vivid dreams of her dad. "Obviously this is because I am wishing he was here to 'sort things out' like he always did," she says.

Her mother suggested, after Rai reported another such dream, that her daughter should simply "let him sort them out!"

"I might just do that," Rai concludes.

Pennies from Heaven

Lori Payne's father Richard passed away in April 2002 and his death was very difficult for both her and her mother. "I was very close to my father and took his loss very hard," Lori says. Soon after Lori's dad died, her mother had a dream in which he came to her, sat on the bed and smiled. The dream provided some relief for Lori's mother, who believed her husband visited her to assure her he was doing well. Lori, however, still struggled with her grief. "I never had that and I *so* wanted to know that he was okay."

Then one afternoon, as Lori and her mother prepared to go out, Mrs. Payne looked down and spotted a penny glinting on the floor. She picked it up and, with a smile, told her daughter, "You realize that when you find a penny, someone from heaven is sending you their love." Lori's mom held up the one-cent piece and said, "I love you, Richard." Though amused by the thought, Lori didn't give it much credence, and off they went on their outing. "I didn't think any more about it."

She has since changed her mind. Almost every day after finding that first penny, Lori has found and still finds pennies on the ground in various locations—at home, at work, on the street, practically everywhere she goes. She always finds the pennies lying heads up. "The first few times I didn't pay attention," she admits. "I would pick them up and go on. Then it struck me that it was happening an awful lot. Maybe my mother is right and Daddy is sending me love." Now, each time she sees yet another penny, she picks it up and tells her father, "I love you too, Daddy."

When you find a penny, be aware that someone from heaven is sending you their love.

The daily penny gives Lori a sense of peace. "Even though Daddy is not physically with us every day, he is still around watching over us. I hope he keeps sending me pennies from heaven." Lori did not hesitate to share her story, and hopes it will help others deal with the loss of a loved one.

Sandor's Visit

Anne Marie Szucs' father-in-law, Sandor, was a larger-than-life man who escaped from Hungary with his wife, Trudy, during the Hungarian Revolution of 1956. The couple settled in Calgary, Alberta, and created a stable, comfortable life for themselves and their two sons.

"When I first met Sandor," Anne Marie reminisces, "I was just a little afraid of his powerful and bluntly honest personality." Anne Marie grew to love this pillar of a man, and also fell for his son Alex. "I saw the loving man under the crusty exterior, the man who would do anything for his family and especially for his wife," she says of Sandor.

Sandor died in the fall of 1998 at the age of 79. His death devastated Trudy. Anne Marie could tell Trudy felt lost. She seemed to be going through life's rituals without any care or concern for them. That year, the family gathered as always for Christmas. Trudy hosted the event, still locked in her grief. "At one point she confided in me that she hadn't even dreamed of him, and desperately wanted to. Any connection just to know he was all right," says Anne Marie.

Christmas Eve dinner, the focal point of the family's traditional celebration, appeared on the surface to be the same as always: roast duck, red cabbage, potatoes, cucumber salad, bread, dessert and wine. Trudy served up a feast for the assembled clan, and in Sandor's place at the head of the table she placed two small, intertwined teddy bears. The stuffed animals were a treasured Valentine's gift from Trudy to her husband. With all the food laid out on the table, Trudy sat in her usual place at the end of the table opposite the little bears. Silently, the family began to eat.

About halfway through the meal, Anne Marie looked up at Trudy and, to her astonishment, saw Sandor standing to Trudy's right, with one arm draped around his wife. She felt as though he radiated a sense of comfort. "I must say that I sensed him more than I saw him," Anne Marie says. "I could see his outline, yet all his features were blurred. But I *knew* it was him," recalls Anne Marie.

Her first reaction was to blame the vision on too much alcohol, but she realized she had drunk only one glass of wine. She looked around the table. Did anyone else see him? Was she going crazy? But sure enough, when she looked back at Trudy, Sandor was still there. Finally, Anne Marie quietly asked Alex to join her in the kitchen for a moment so she could speak to him. She told him what she had seen and asked for his advice: should she tell Trudy or would this kind of news upset her even more? Alex surprised Anne Marie by accepting her vision of his father without question. He encouraged her to tell his mother.

"We went back to the table," says Anne Marie. "I could still sense Sandor there. I felt a little strange about it all, but I told Trudy what I was seeing."

The news brought an immediate reaction. "Really? Where is he?" Trudy asked excitedly.

Anne Marie told her mother-in-law that Sandor stood right beside her. "A light came on in her that I hadn't seen in months."

Sandor's visit left a lasting impression on Trudy, unlocking her from the grip of overwhelming grief. Several nights later, she dreamed of her husband for the first time since his death. He was sitting in a garden. She asked him, "Where are you? Are you happy?" He told her everything was fine and that he had just enjoyed tea with two British gentlemen. Months later, in her second dream of Sandor, Trudy asked him if he had been with the family at Christmas. He replied, "Yes."

Anne Marie says her mother-in-law now asks at every Christmas whether or not Sandor is present. He has not shown himself since that first visit, but Anne Marie often senses his presence, making sure his wife and family are all right. "I don't know why I was the only one who saw him that night," she says, "but it was a gift. To all of us."

A Mother's Spirit Checks In

Roland's mother died when he was 12, though he didn't find out about it until two weeks after her death. He only knew that his mother, for some unexplained reason, did not come home one night. Though that may seem strange, Roland's mother was often away and he and his younger sister were accustomed to being home alone. They didn't think much about her absence for the first day or two. It was summer, school was closed for the holidays, and they managed fairly well. They couldn't go outside to play, however, because their mother insisted they stay in while she was away.

On their third day alone, Roland stood in the kitchen looking out the back door at the other neighborhood children running around, while his sister sat on the floor and amused herself with a doll. As he stood at the door, he noticed something out of the corner of his eye. "When I looked, I saw this really bright light pulsating and floating across the room. It floated over my sister's head, right by me, and through the wall." Roland was so convinced of what he had seen that he immediately scanned outside the window to see if the light had emerged on the other side.

Eventually, he and his sister learned the reason behind their mother's absence. He never thought about the light again until many years later when he happened to catch a television program about true encounters with spirits. Video footage showed orbs, or floating balls of light, much like the one Roland witnessed in the kitchen as a child. It didn't sink in right away, but after seeing other shows with documented evidence of spiritual presence, he suddenly realized what he had seen. "I now believe that the floating light I saw was the spirit of my mother coming by to check on us," Roland states on the website GhostVillage.com, where this story first appeared. "I am the type of person that only believes what I see, so that event made me a believer in life of some form after death."

The Scent of a Father

Qulia Goodman's family believes that anyone who dies will be greeted on the other side by a family member, a sort of guardian spirit guide to the next plane. When her father had a heart attack and was admitted into hospital, her mother told Qulia that he wouldn't pull through. She said that Qulia's deceased aunt—her father's sister—had arrived in spirit and her father had spoken to her.

"He lived a few short days, but nobody expected him to come out of it," says Qulia. "Everyone basically accepted the fact that Aunt D. had come to lead him over to the other side."

The Goodmans also believe that "the spirits of our loved ones who have crossed over are free to go wherever they choose and do whatever they wish," Qulia says. "I've never heard anyone actually explain why they believe this. It's just taken for granted." The result is exemplified in the following story.

Qulia's mother and father were married in 1934. Her father died in 1988. A few years later, her mother grew very ill and stayed at Qulia's house so she could be monitored. "I had her camped out on my sofa, where I could watch her constantly," says Qulia.

One afternoon, as Qulia sat in the chair beside her mother, she received a visit from "Daddy." This wasn't Qulia's first encounter with her father's spirit; her harrowing experience in a car accident when she heard her father's voice appears earlier in this book. This time, however, the experience was a more subtle visitation. Qulia's father was a mechanic who dipped Levi Garnett snuff. He carried a particular scent, or combination of scents, that the entire family recognized.

That afternoon, as she cared for her mother, Qulia suddenly smelled her father. "He was right there with me." And just as suddenly, she realized that her mother needed to be taken to the hospital.

"I don't know how long he was there because it seemed like things were moving in slow motion at that particular time. But as soon as the scent was gone, I knew exactly what to do." She called her brother to come over and take care of her children, then she put her mother in the car and headed for the emergency room.

It turned out that her mother had pneumonia and required treatments to clear her lungs. Although the condition wasn't life-threatening, it was serious because of her age. "So I believe—and she does, too—that after 54 years of marriage, he was still looking after her," says Qulia of her father's intervention. "She's getting ready to turn 86 now, and I think he still looks after her."

Qulia's parents had 10 children; she is the youngest. Not long ago, one of her sisters came to visit and they talked about their father's ongoing guardian spirit role. Qulia's sister admitted that sometimes when she's alone, she'll hear a truck pull into her driveway and the door slam shut. When she investigates, there is no one there. "She said that it sounds just like Daddy's old truck and that she feels like he's come to visit," says Qulia. "Just to check up on her and make sure she's okay. I believe her."

Granddad's Gift

Dave Gotcher receives guidance and support from his maternal and paternal grandfathers, both of whom died many years ago when he was a child. In this story, he recalls the first time the spirit of his grandpa, James Gotcher, made Dave aware of its presence and literally kept him from falling on his head. Dave was only a small child at the time of this incident, but his memory of his grandfather's protective spirit remains with him, vivid and reassuring.

Born on the West Coast of the United States, Dave grew up primarily in the Los Angeles area, though his family traveled a lot because his father served in the US Navy. When Dave was about five years old, his family moved back to California from Florida, and passed through Texas to visit his father's family on the way. Dave only met his Grandpa Gotcher twice while he was alive. "This was the last time I ever really saw my grandfather in the flesh," Dave tells me.

The Gotchers eventually reached California and moved into their new house. Dave shared a room with his younger brother and, being the eldest child, claimed the top bunk. One night, not long after moving in, Dave dreamed that he rolled out of bed and started to fall to the hardwood floor. Dave remembers the dream to this day. "As I fell, a man caught me. He was solid and warm and smelled like cherry tobacco. He had on a denim shirt and jeans. He held me close to his chest and just said, "Eeeeeasy there" and laughed as he laid me on the floor."

The tobacco-scented rescuer tussled Dave's hair and then faded from view.

The next morning Dave's mother found him asleep on the floor. When she asked how he got down there, Dave told her about falling out of bed and the man who caught him. His mother assumed it was just a dream.

A few days later, Dave's father packed up to leave. This was nothing new given his work in the navy, but even as a child Dave noticed his mother was more sad than usual. "When I asked her what was wrong she said that my grandpa on my dad's side had died a few days earlier and Dad was going to the funeral," Dave says. "I told her I felt bad because I couldn't recall what he looked like. We'd been spending so much time with her own dad that he had become the only grandpa I could picture."

Dave's mom found a photo of Grandpa Gotcher and when she showed it to her son, he immediately recognized the man that had been in his room. "I told her that was the man who caught me when I fell out of bed the other night. Of course it turns out that was the night he passed away."

The story remained a secret between Dave and his mother. His mom thought it best not to tell his father, who didn't believe in that sort of thing. She, however, was convinced when Dave told her about the cherry tobacco smell. She admitted to Dave that his grandfather smoked a pipe, but never in front of the kids. "It was one of the very few secrets I ever kept from my father," says Dave.

After that initial encounter, the spirit of Dave's paternal grandfather often gave him a sense of confidence and security when his father was at sea. To this day, he senses the presence of both his grandfathers. Over the years, their spiritual guidance taught Dave to be more lighthearted and less solemn. "I was a very serious child," Dave explains. His maternal grandfather, Howard Lee, helps him "keep a keen sense of whimsy." And every so often, he gets a feeling of strength and attributes it to his Grandpa Gotcher. It leaves Dave feeling both lucky and blessed to be on the receiving end of such a remarkable gift.

The Other Side of the Family

What makes some people more susceptible to seeing or experiencing guardian angels than others? No one knows for sure but the ability often seems to run in the family. Andrew Schuster can trace his family's heritage, and connection to spirits, back several generations to the small town of St. Felicien, Quebec. Andrew, for the record, is first cousin of Brenda Walsh, whose stories of her side of the family also appear in this book.

In 1914, Andrew's grandmother, Marie Aurelia, fell through the ice of the North Saskatchewan River while skating one winter day. Her father managed to save her from drowning, but she contracted pneumonia and almost died. During the worst time in her illness, Aurelia reported seeing a large rosary and feeling the urge to climb the beads as if they were a stairway. Her mother's voice called to her from what seemed like a great distance and Aurelia could not answer, but she didn't ascend the rosary staircase. Eventually she recovered from her condition, though recurring bouts of pneumonia plagued her for many years after. Were angels present? It is impossible to say. But the link to the spiritual world of guardian angels strengthened in Aurelia's children and grandchildren.

Aurelia's daughter (and Andrew's mother) Bèrénice was only three months old when her Grandfather Tremblay lay on his deathbed. Aurelia took Bèrénice to the ailing man and helped her form a sign of the cross on his head, saying that he had been blessed by a little angel and could now die in peace. He died soon after.

Bèrénice heard this story many times as she grew up and Andrew suggests that perhaps this explains his mother's lifelong fondness for angels. She lived with cancer the last eight years of her life and during this time often reflected on death. Bèrénice relied on her family but also maintained a strong belief in angels and turned to them during difficult times. Through prayer, she developed a relationship with three angels that she believed to be manifestations of her mother (died 1951), her brother Robert (died 1984) and her brother Bill (died 1991). As she neared her own death, or what she called "the end of her ruler," she began to receive visits from her angels.

Over the course of one week not long before her death, all three angels appeared to Bèrénice. The first visit, which she believed to be from her brother Bill, occurred one morning when she was feeling rather low and eating breakfast in the kitchen. The sun had not yet crested the horizon, but a radiant light suddenly illuminated the kitchen and filled Bèrénice with a sense of peace. The second visit took place that afternoon. This time Bèrénice believed the angel to be her brother Robert. While resting in her comfortable chair in the living room, Bèrénice thought she heard something, then felt a presence in the room and a chill run down her spine. The last visit came at night while she slept. She dreamed of her mother, who promised her she would return when it was time for Bèrénice to join her.

"My mother had a close and unique relationship with all of her children, including me," says Andrew, the youngest of Bèrénice Schuster's nine children. When doctor's diagnosed her with cancer in 1994, Bèrénice was living in a small community in Alberta. Andrew lived an hour away in Edmonton.

The prospect of eventually losing his mother to cancer affected Andrew very early on, and he prepared himself for difficult times ahead. "During these years I spent as much time with my mother as I could while she continued to cope with cancer in her life." Bèrénice often stayed with Andrew in Edmonton while she received radiation and chemotherapy treatments at the Cross Cancer Clinic. The treatments were difficult, but Andrew appreciated having time to spend alone with his mother.

Andrew recalls that time as a special opportunity to share experiences, dreams, aspirations and love with his mother. Bèrénice recounted stories from her childhood and remembered things she cherished. She was particularly fond of Disney movies; her father had often treated his children to trips to see newly released films such as *Cinderella* and *Snow White*. "My mother told me that she particularly liked the two chipmunk characters," says Andrew. That revelation would come to be much more significant than he anticipated.

Bèrénice also told him the poignant story of the last time she saw her mother prior to Aurelia's death. Aurelia stood looking out the window of her house. It was December 27, 1951, and the newly married Bèrénice was leaving her mother to start a life with her husband. Bèrénice's mother waved goodbye, as she always did when one of her children departed. No one could have predicted it would be a final farewell. Aurelia died on January 30 of a heart condition that she had kept hidden from the family. "Given my mother's foreseeable death, this image stuck with me," Andrew recalls. He wondered with some dread when he would last see her.

Meanwhile, Andrew had considered pursuing a post-graduate degree for over a decade. He delayed this pursuit for many reasons, but in early 2001 he decided to apply to graduate business programs in Vancouver and Edmonton. At the same time, Andrew met a new partner who lived in Vancouver. As the months passed and the relationship deepened, Andrew's desire to live in the same city as his partner grew stronger. When he was accepted as a student at the University of British Columbia, his decision was made. Though sad to leave his mother, he moved to Vancouver to be with his partner and continue his career.

In Vancouver, Andrew lived in a condominium complex overlooking the stunning Van Dusen Gardens. "From my third floor view, the high branches of the trees were at eye level," he explains. He found himself staring frequently out the windows of his apartment at the trees. "It was common to see squirrels scampering along branches, jumping from tree to tree," he remembers, "and these animals were reminiscent of the Disney chipmunk characters

The squirrels were reminiscent of the Disney chipmunk characters Andrew's mother adored.

that my mom adored." His reveries frequently led Andrew to think of his mother in Edmonton.

Bèrénice's condition deteriorated quickly after Andrew left. On February 16, 2002, she succumbed to the long ordeal, with several of her children at her side. When they realized she had passed on, they began the difficult process of notifying other siblings.

When his phone rang, Andrew immediately knew why. "As I answered it, one of the squirrels that had always kept its distance high in the trees appeared on my patio," he recalls. "The bushy-tailed squirrel came right up to the patio window immediately in front of me and stopped to peer inside."

Andrew received the news of his mother's death, and tears welled up in his eyes. Observing him, the squirrel turned and hopped up on the edge of the patio wall, stopped and peered over its shoulder. Andrew felt drawn to the animal. "It waited. I waved goodbye and the squirrel hopped forward. It stopped and looked over its shoulder one more time, then disappeared back into the forest.

"There is no doubt in my mind that the squirrel was a sign from my mother. It was too coincidental to be otherwise." It may have been her way of letting him know she still watched over him, and allowing him to wave goodbye for the last time.

Much earlier in his life, Andrew encountered a guardian spirit who literally shadowed him to keep him safe. It happened during the early 1980s, when he studied engineering at the University of Alberta.

"I lived with my grandparents at that time. I would commute back and forth by bicycle as a way of saving money and keeping fit. It was a time to turn off my brain from a hard day at university, and after traveling this route many times the journey home became very familiar and didn't require much attention," says Andrew. The ride flew by, and some days he felt he arrived home before he knew he had even left the university.

In April 1983, during Andrew's second year of university, his grandfather died. His death occurred at the end of a school term, when Andrew was in the habit of studying into the wee hours to complete the year's work and prepare for exams.

On one particular evening Andrew returned home very late. It was dark; the street lights gave a patchy view of the road ahead. He cycled along Jasper Avenue heading toward the city's west end. As he passed the street lights, his shadow grew in front of him until he approached the next light. Then the shadow would reverse and move backward until he passed the next streetlight, and so on.

As he neared an intersection, a second shadow appeared and joined his own. He assumed another late-night cyclist was behind him, perhaps also on his way home. "But the shadow got closer and closer to my own shadow," says Andrew. "It seemed the cyclist was getting very near to me and made me very uncomfortable." Andrew turned right and took the opportunity to peer behind and ask the other cyclist to pass. Andrew couldn't believe his eyes. "There was nobody there."

For the rest of the trip his solitary shadow remained. Dumbfounded, he cycled the rest of the way home, convinced that something very strange had just happened.

Several days later, Andrew found himself back in that same spot where the second shadow appeared. Unlike most days, when he cycled home with his mind on autopilot, he felt unusually alert. "I couldn't help but remember the odd incident and was somewhat on edge."

Suddenly, a car accelerated past Andrew and made an abrupt right-hand turn in front of him. Andrew grabbed his brakes just in time. In doing so, he avoided being hit in front of the car, and instead ran into the side of the vehicle. He flew up onto the car, which then stopped.

Andrew walked away from the accident unharmed but quite shaken. "If I'd been in one of my regular stupors, I might have been seriously injured or worse," says Andrew. He is sure the shadow cyclist was an omen from beyond this world. "I believe it was my grandfather's spirit warning me."

5
Guidance from Beyond

∾

*"The delight of the
wisdom of the angels is to
communicate to others
what they know."*

—Emmanuel Swedenborg

∾

Go East!

In August 1989, while living in Richmond, British Columbia, Judith Munns had a remarkable experience. She now lives on Vancouver Island and shared this story as just one example of how her guardian angel affected the course of her life.

She was lying on her bed one day, eyes closed, meditating and praying, when suddenly she heard a loud "pop" followed by a sound similar to paper tearing. Startled, she opened her eyes to see a bright light shining through what appeared to be a crack in the air below the ceiling of her bedroom. "As I watched, the crack of light lengthened, turned a right angle in the air above me, and turned again and again, forming a perfect rectangle suspended in the air just below my ceiling," says Judith. "Then, with another cracking sound, a line of light suddenly split the middle, and the apparition became a window, which opened upward," says Judith.

Light streamed down through the open window, flooding Judith with an incredible feeling of love, warmth and peace. In the window above her she could see an angel standing with arms held upward, its wings fluttering a little over its shoulders. Many other angels hovered in the background. Overwhelmed, Judith did not notice whether they were male or female; such a detail did not matter at the time.

The angel spoke to her, offering one simple instruction: "Go east." Judith replied, as if she knew exactly what this meant, "Oh! It's *time* then!" The angel smiled and said, "Yes, it is."

Judith then asked, "Why do you appear to me in this form?" The angel seemed momentarily confused but, as Judith explains, "It then understood that I 'knew' that angels were pure light, and I had always seen them that way. At that moment the facade of face, hands, wings, seemed to float in front of an even brighter light. Then the facade dissipated, and for a fraction of a moment I was bathed in pure light, pure love." The visit ended as abruptly as it began. The light moved backward as the "window" closed and disappeared with an audible *snap*.

Judith stayed still on her bed, feeling the angels' incredible love surround her. Then she began to speak to the angels. She told them that she was ready, but that the recommendation to "go east" was a little vague. She did not know what her next step would be, or that the angels would lead her in the right direction.

For the next three months, Judith says she felt a loving aura around everything she did, said and experienced. Then, in late November, her life changed overnight. "My husband at the time was bipolar, or as we said in those days, manic depressive. In the midst of an episode, he became violent, putting me in the hospital," she says. Her husband, a lawyer, was arrested and taken to the same jail where he worked as duty counsel. "It is important that you know that throughout the whole experience, I felt only overwhelming love toward him, and *knew* that this was something we both had agreed to, before we ever came into this life," Judith stresses. "At no time did I ever feel victimized or angry about what had happened."

Judith's husband's altruism and willingness to assist people who could not pay had led him to serve as a legal aid lawyer. The morning after his arrest, he appeared before the judge for whom he had worked the previous six years. The judge told him to stay six city blocks away from his wife or risk jail.

Since the couple not only shared a home but also worked in the same office, it seemed easier at the time for Judith to work from home until "things returned to normal." However, a week later, Judith's secretary called from the office with bad news. Judith's husband had forgotten to tell her that the owners of the house they leased had informed him three months before that they were returning from their sabbatical, and would move back into their home on December 15. "I had less than two weeks to vacate the house," Judith recalls. Rather than fret, Judith realized this was her opportunity to "go east."

Just as quickly as the angels appeared three months before, Judith found herself traveling in northeastern British Columbia and northern Alberta. She spent the next four years working jobs and living in situations that mysteriously manifested and just as mysteriously dissolved. "There were many mornings when I did not even know what city I would be living in that night. Everywhere I went, I felt guided, protected and loved," says Judith.

Her experiences taught her the most important lessons of her life. "I learned that God truly is in every situation, every heart, every moment, and that the only power I have is in this moment. I learned to trust implicitly that my every need will be taken care of. During those four years, I was never without a warm bed, money in my pocket, gas in my Bronco and love in my heart."

Judith also felt protected at all times. On one occasion, she had a car accident in -40° F weather. There was no visible damage to her vehicle so she drove on another 160 miles. "And then, without even a warning wobble, a tire came off its hub one hour after I got to my destination, while my vehicle was parked outside my parents' home."

After four years, her husband died of an aneurism alone in his Richmond home. "It was clear to me that our work together was finally done, and he could move on, giving me freedom to move on to the next part of my 'work' in this life," says Judith. In 1993, she married an old friend she used to work with. "Our life together is loving, blessed, rich with joy and peace and, above all, we continue to be service oriented."

While some angelic messages offer immediate guidance through hazardous or difficult situations, Judith benefited from a simple yet profound message that continues to have an effect on her life.

Mary's Many Angels

In desperate times, Mary Shaffer knows that guardian angels wait in the wings, so to speak, ready to help. She now counts her husband among the spirits that watch over her, but her experiences began decades ago. From her home in Wisconsin, she told me of several encounters that marked the path of her life.

Back when Mary's children were in their teens, personal problems threatened to overwhelm her. She felt alienated, without anyone in whom she could confide. "I was desperate and depressed," she remembers. One morning as she lay in bed, unwilling to face another day of despair, Mary noticed something standing in her room. "I saw some crossed arms in white and the Eucharist in the center of the hands. I saw no head, no legs and no wings, but I did receive a feeling of calmness, peace and comfort, a sense that I could handle things. From then on I just knew that *someone* knew what was going on and that I was cared for."

A second incident convinced her that the first vision had been neither random nor ridiculous. While driving from Canada to Buffalo, New York, Mary found herself in a sudden snowstorm. It was night, and blinding snow impaired her vision and made the roads nearly impassable. Drifting snow had reduced the road to one lane of traffic. "I couldn't see anything," she recalls. "So I prayed really hard and kept driving slowly. Suddenly a car appeared in front of me. I could just make out its taillights and I followed it back to civilization." Once she reached the suburbs, Mary made her way home, guided by street lights. Only later did she realize her unknown savior must have been heaven sent. "I'm not sure where the car came from but it hadn't been there before and suddenly it was in front of me. The thing is, there was no access road for it to pull out from. If a car had come onto that road it would have had to be behind me and with all the snow there wasn't room to pass." Once she reached the city lights, Mary knew she could find her way home and consequently didn't notice where the car went. But the experience deepened her belief in her guardian angel guides. After a few such experiences, she says, "you get to believe that these things really do happen."

While working as a nurse at an infirmary run by nuns, Mary received another reminder of the angels' presence. As she made her rounds one day she came across a patient's room that sat empty and had been closed for a long time. She felt it needed some fresh air, and so she opened the door. From the doorway, she could see through the windows, which looked out onto the hospital grounds. But what caught her attention was the light of a bright, white cross that filled the whole window. "It shone through like a street light, but there were no lights outside. I was impressed and wondered where it came from. It had never been there before. I had cared for patients in that room and no light ever shone like that." Mary decided the light had special meaning, and closed the door again.

One day she watched as one of the nuns opened the door, did a double take and quickly shut the door again. Though she never spoke of it, Mary knew the woman had also seen the remarkable light. In the end, the light

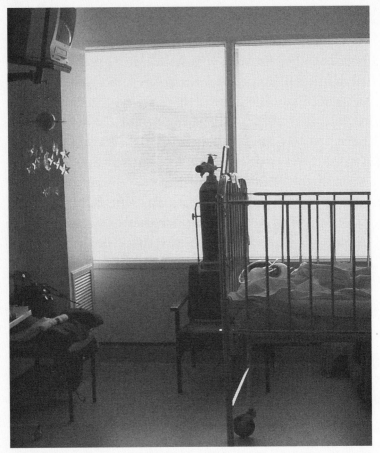

It shone through like a street light, but there were no lights outside... I had cared for patients in that room and no light ever shone like that.

remained a mystery, but Mary took it as a sign that angels are not shy about visiting.

Then in May 1993, Mary's husband Dennis died of a heart attack. Soon after the funeral, Mary started hearing strange noises in the house, like the sound of doors closing and footsteps in the hall. "The first time I thought,

'What was that?' Then I knew exactly what that sound was. My husband was heavy and had arthritis so he walked with a heavy foot. I could hear the distinct sound of him walking around the house." Mary admits the sounds unnerved her at first, but after the first visit, she grew accustomed to having her husband's spirit around, "checking in." On another occasion, the song they played on their honeymoon came floating out of the car radio when she went to run some errands. She took it as a sign from Dennis, assuring her that he was all right.

The first New Year's Eve after Dennis' death, Mary sensed her husband in the room. "I had worked until 11 PM and when I got home, I sat in the chair by the door to relax. The whole family was around, coming and going, and everyone was talking. Suddenly, it felt like someone opened and closed the front door. A very cold chill wrapped around my legs. No one else felt it. I don't know, but I just had the sensation that Dennis was there with me." Mary chose not to share her experience with her family at the time, though she is certain that Dennis' spirit came to check up on her.

These days, Mary no longer hears the noises, but still feels Dennis' presence. Until recently, however, she hadn't told anyone about her experiences with guardian angels and with her husband's spirit.

"I never mentioned this before because who can you really tell? You don't drop this all of a sudden on people," she says. "When something is so powerful and strange, you don't know what to do with it. But you also don't care about sharing it because it is so wonderful."

Listening to Angels

Angels rarely make physical appearances, but they can make their presence known in other ways, like sending warm sensations and noises that defy human description. In *Angel Talk: Are You Listening,* Robert Graham suggests that everyone has guardian angels willing to communicate with them, but most people are too preoccupied to listen. He maintains that by being attentive and open to this communication, we can hear the angels' messages. "Angels are polite and have strict orders not to interfere in our daily lives," he writes, "except in dire circumstances. They will, however, drop subtle messages to keep us out of trouble if we are alert enough to catch them."

Mary Stevenson decided to tune in to her guardian angels a few years ago and took a workshop called "Listening to your Angels." As a hypnotherapist and Reiki Master, Mary anticipated the information from the workshop would assist her with her clients by opening her to other channels of communication. Throughout the three-day course, Mary felt the presence of her angels. "I'm very intuitive. Right away I tuned into angels around me. They were quite lighthearted with me, joking and giving me poems with messages, but nothing serious," she says. The angelic messages suggested she take life easier and not be so hard on herself. "I was going through a difficult personal time, so they were telling me to find the humor in life." She left the workshop feeling that it had been interesting, but hadn't inspired any life-altering communication with the angels.

Soon after completing the course, Mary's friend Barb (whose name has been changed to protect her family's privacy) received upsetting medical news. Barb's physician diagnosed her with aggressive abdominal cancer. The news came as a shock—she had survived breast cancer at 17 years old and now, at 30, the disease's recurrence looked ominous. Barb confided in Mary about the cancer and her fears, and Mary told her about the angel workshop she'd attended. Barb then asked if Mary might request some information from the angels.

That night, Mary sat down, "tuned in" and asked for information for her friend. In Graham's *Angel Talk,* he points out that in order to receive a clear message from angels, one must ask a direct question. Angels will always answer questions; the more concise and clear the question, the more tangible and explicit the answer. Mary worked through her own angels to reach two angels close to Barb. "I go into a meditation and tune into the person's soul energy and speak with them at a higher level," Mary explains. "The angels come in my mind's eye. I never physically see them."

Mary's questions about Barb generated immediate results. "Right away they started to communicate with me and gave me some very valuable information regarding issues that my friend needed to look at so she could heal her body and soul. They were very specific about one family member towards whom Barb felt a lot of anger. The angels said she really needed to confront the unresolved anger."

Mary called Barb and recounted all the information the angels gave her. "There was silence on the other end of the phone," says Mary. "She thanked me and hung up." After a week, Barb called again to ask if Mary would be willing to communicate with the angels once more. Barb didn't explain her feelings in great detail but said that the angels had been correct in their first assessment. She was struggling with issues she had with someone very close to her, and knew she had to make peace with this person before she could move on. She would either heal herself or pass on into the next life with unresolved issues. Once again Mary contacted Barb's angels and relayed the information. According to the angels, the urgent need for Barb to address the conflict persisted.

For a time, the messages helped Barb find a way to cope with her anger, and her cancer went into remission. But the reprieve was short lived. Mary says her friend couldn't divest herself completely of her fury toward the other person. The cancer returned within a few weeks.

Mary continued to communicate with Barb's angels until Barb's death three months later. "I know their messages brought her peace and I think that's why they were present in my life so strongly for those few months," Mary says of the experience. "Interestingly enough, I have not communicated with them since."

High-flying Help

Even people who seek help for their addictions will often find their spirits weakened. In those moments, the decision between staying the course and abandoning it completely becomes very difficult, as one young military flight engineer discovered. But just as his resolve seemed ready to disintegrate, he received unexpected and otherworldly encouragement that guided him through the rough patch. My thanks to Rowena and the Australian website castleofspirits.com for permission to include this story in this collection.

The story was originally told by David Clement, a friend of the flight engineer who I'll call Don. Don served as an onboard mechanic/navigator with the Canadian military, which he had joined at a young age.

During one trip to an extremely remote area in Canada's Far North, Don struggled to stay focused on his work. His mind was preoccupied and in turmoil over some personal issues, and the stress began to affect him. He wanted a drink, even though he had resisted alcohol for some time, aware of his dangerous addiction. When the plane landed on the narrow runway strip, Don had already leaped ahead in his mind to the welcoming mess hall where the crew would meet to debrief after the flight.

Once inside the hall, Don edged closer to giving in to temptation. In this remote place, who would know if he had a few drinks? He decided to have a cocktail or two during the debriefing session, despite the obvious consequences. He sat down, ready to order, but just as he was about to place his drink request, a captain he had never met sat down next to him and introduced himself as "a friend of Bill's." Don immediately recognized the identification code used by members of Alcoholics Anonymous.

Surprised but somewhat relieved, Don realized that he really needed someone to talk to about his worries, someone to offer support through this personal crisis. He and the captain spoke for a while. At the end of the conversation, the captain gave Don his name and contact details, then told him to go find his AA book and read up on the step in the program that addressed relapses.

Don followed the captain's suggestion. The book's encouragement combined with his long talk with the captain made his craving for a drink fade. He returned to the mess hall to thank the captain, but the man had disappeared. Don tried to find him, using the contact information he had been given, but the administrative staff at the bases the captain listed on his contact information told Don they had never heard of the man. He didn't exist in any of the records.

Everyone in the mess hall admitted observing the man who spoke to Don, but no one had ever seen him before, which struck Don as odd given the isolated location. He was left wondering whether the captain was really a guardian angel or spirit sent to help a man in need before he made a terrible mistake.

Message in Mexico

The exhilaration of travel to exotic locales sometimes obscures its risks. While marveling at unique historic sites and landscapes, it is easy to forget our vulnerability to those with less than hospitable intentions. One couple from Edmonton, Alberta, realized only in hindsight that a protective spirit guided them out of harm's way while they traveled in Mexico.

In 1989, Janet and Philip MacLellan made the long drive south to Mexico City to visit the shrine of Our Lady of Guadalupe. They wanted to join the 10 million people who visit the popular pilgrimage site each year. Set on a hill at Tepeyac, northwest of Mexico City, the enormous basilica holds the *tilma,* a rough cactus cloth worn in 1531 by the poor Aztec Juan Diego. As the story goes, a "lady from heaven" appeared to Diego and identified herself as the Mother of the True God. She told Diego to instruct the bishop to build a temple on the site, and as proof of her presence she left an image of herself miraculously imprinted on Diego's peasant robe.

Today, the Lady of Guadalupe has been attributed with an extensive and astonishing list of miracles. Scientists still can't explain the origin of the image on the cloth, or why its crude fiber has not decayed in more than 470 years.

After seeing the incredible shrine, the MacLellans were soon ready to leave the country. "It was very hot," recalls Janet. "We were tired of the heat and decided to head home early." Seasoned travelers, the couple knew that bandits made some areas of the country unsafe for tourists, but they had checked with the Mexican consulate before planning their trip and felt prepared. What they weren't prepared for was simple navigational errors. On their way to the Mexican-American border, they got lost.

"We were driving around the small town of Matamoros and could not find our way to the border," says Janet. "We stopped several times to ask for directions but were greeted with the same response each time: 'No speak English.' " Janet and her husband grew frustrated and somewhat fearful as they realized night would soon fall and no one was willing to help.

Then, while stopped at a red light, they noticed a car with an English "For Sale" sign in the window. On instinct, Janet rolled down her window and called to the male driver to get his attention. She asked if he knew how to get to the border and he replied, "Follow me." They followed the man for some time, but grew nervous as he led them through "some pretty shady-looking parts of the town."

As they passed through the downtown area and drove out to an outlying area past the houses, Philip commented that he feared the guy was taking them "for a ride," and that they were following him right into a trap. But just as Janet's husband declared, "We've got to lose him," the man stopped and pointed toward the border. Both Janet and Philip turned in the direction the man pointed and realized he had shown them a safe passage.

Philip turned to wave and thank their guide, but both the guide and the car had disappeared. "There was nowhere for it to go," says Janet. "It was just open road around us. There were no alleys to duck down or houses to hide behind." Janet was still focused on the border and unaware of the strange development. Her husband didn't tell her that their mysterious guide had inexplicably vanished until some time later, when they were well on their way home.

Janet grew up believing in guardian angels and has always felt protected by them. Recently, when she needed to wake up for an appointment, she heard a female voice rouse her by calling her name. Since her husband passed away in April 2002 and she doesn't own an alarm clock, she is certain it was a guardian angel ensuring she got out of bed in time. But the experience in Mexico remains Janet's most concrete evidence of the guardian angels watching over her.

A Lifetime of Angels

Angels always have been part of Verna Schmidt's life. The first prayer she and her nine siblings learned was a prayer to their guardian angels. Her mother declared with a farmer's practicality that she couldn't keep an eye on all ten of them on the farm, and instead asked the guardian angels to watch over her brood. She also thought it important that her children learn to talk to the angels on their own.

Verna says, "I remember her saying, 'Don't make a federal case out of your request; just tell them what you need. They know anyway, but it is good to get in the habit of asking.' So we asked."

The sensible Schmidt clan asked the angels to keep the milking cows from kicking them and to keep their horse-drawn hayrack from tipping over on the hilly land they farmed in Alberta. "But we also asked for things that would not have met with my parents' approval," says Verna. "We asked for the courage to climb furthest up the hip roof of the old barn before jumping to the ground below. Or to make sure that we had impeccable balance so that we would not touch the ground as we played our game of See Who Can Make it Around the Entire Farmyard Without Ever Touching the Ground." Angel protection was a crucial part of this game, which involved leaping from the rooftop of the milk house to the pump house some four feet away.

Verna herself harbored an intense fear of bulls, having been chased by one as a child. She therefore always invoked her angels when it was her turn to retrieve the cows, especially when the bull was in the same pasture.

"I can't say I ever saw an angel in my childhood but there was not a trace of doubt that they were with me."

Verna received her first message from her angel on a day she now calls The Soup Day. She recalls, "I was late arriving home from work. We needed groceries. My son had a hockey game across town. I wanted him to eat something before we left. My plan was to put on a pot of soup and then get groceries." In her haste to prepare everything before the hockey game, she put the soup pot on the stove and set the burner to high, intending to bring it to a boil then turn the heat down before leaving to buy groceries. Instead, she turned it on high and walked out the door.

She was at the grocery store about five blocks from home when she heard someone calling her name. "I looked behind me in the aisle but no one else was there," recounts Verna. "I continued my shopping and again I heard 'Verna,' only this time with an edge of urgency to it. I looked up and down the aisle and even peered between the cans to the other side. I was beginning to feel a little irritated since I didn't have time to play games with anyone."

Again she heard her name called, only this time the voice demanded attention. There in the middle of the grocery store she shouted back, "What?! What do you want?" much to the amazement of the startled senior citizen beside her.

The voice softened and replied, "I want you to remember that you left the soup on."

"Oh my God, the soup!" she screamed, abandoning her grocery cart and heading for the door.

Her heart pounded as she sprinted to her car. All those childhood years spent learning to communicate with her guardian angel finally paid off. "Guardian angel," she pronounced, "I need you to make sure that I don't start a fire in the house."

Driving far beyond reasonable speed, Verna suddenly sensed energy in the car. She glanced over to the passenger seat. "I didn't see anything. I did feel the tension in me start to drain and hear a gentle voice saying, 'It's okay. Slow down. I called you in time.'"

She rushed into the house to find that she had indeed been called in time. The soup had boiled down to a final ring of liquid near the pot's warped bottom.

Verna has heard or sensed her angel's guidance several times since that day. "A second incident that I hold dear to my heart occurred one weekend when my husband Dennis and I went camping in order to try out his new fishing boat." They picked the boat up on their way out of the city. After setting up their tent trailer, they launched the boat. But a fractious motor stalled their enthusiasm. Countless pulls later, the motor finally fired. They had time for only a short trip around the west side of the lake before dark.

Dennis anchored the boat onshore. Then, concerned about leaving it there, he took the motor off and hauled it up to the campsite. Verna says, "I told him not to worry. Since we were in a somewhat remote area and had taken both the motor and the oars, it was unlikely anyone would bother with our little fishing boat." Unfortunately, she was wrong.

The next morning a cry of anguish broke the still air. The boat was gone. The boat they had owned for a few hours was nowhere to be seen. Verna and Dennis soon realized it hadn't just drifted away; the iron anchor was gone as well. They scoured the lake edge and nearby forest, hoping that someone just took it for a joy ride and then abandoned it. There was no sign of the boat, only some tire tracks leading down to a beach area a little farther away.

Dennis was angry, at himself and at Verna for convincing him not to worry the night before. Verna took matters into her own hands. "I went to the water's edge to talk to my angel. 'You promised me I could call on you, and now I need help. I need you to help me find Dennis' boat.' And as I opened my eyes the sun caught some metal at the other side of the lake. I knew it was the boat."

"It's on the other side of the lake." Verna told Dennis.

"How would you know that?" he taunted. "You can barely see halfway across the lake."

"It's there because my angel showed me where it is." Verna assured him. "See, just watch. The sun will catch it and then you'll see it too." Luckily, her angel was paying attention. The sun caught the metal again and Dennis saw the flash of light. He waited for the flash to occur again so he could determine the boat's location. It didn't.

They drove to the other side of the lake and tried to find a place where they could reach the lakeshore. Eventually, Verna sensed that they should park the car and head down to the lake through a pasture. They crested a small hill before the animals came into view. To Verna's terror, not one but two bulls stood chewing their cud in the morning sunshine. "I told Dennis I couldn't go through that pasture no matter what so he went on without me and I returned to the car. He was back in a few minutes with the good news that the boat had been found."

Dennis' not-so-good news was that he needed Verna to carry the oars while he carried the motor. Once Verna overcame her fear of the bulls, they walked through the pasture to the boat and attached the motor. Dennis then informed her that if the motor started he wouldn't want to turn it off, and she would have to walk back through the field alone.

"I wanted that motor to fire so that I could tear back across that pasture before sunning time was over," Verna recalls. "I prayed, 'Angels, you know what I need even before I do. I need 10,000 of you on this motor so that it goes with the first pull.' The motor caught with the first pull. I was already running, hoping that those critters wouldn't get up quickly to see what the noise was about."

The bulls, however, stood and headed toward the shoreline. Verna's fear sent a shot of adrenaline through her body. "It is hard to remember that you have an angel that can handle any safety issue when your body is on fire with fear. Good thing angels take action in those cases, as my angel did. I heard it say, 'It's okay, Verna, I stand between you and them. Trust!'

"I trusted, but my legs ran anyway!"

Jason's Message

Raymond pointed out at the beginning of our conversation that he was both a biochemist with the Canadian Department of National Defence and a dyed-in-the-wool agnostic when he came face-to-face with his guardian spirit. "It completely rocked my world," he told me. "I thought I was having a psychotic episode." Far from a synaptic malfunction, what Raymond experienced altered the course of his life and transformed his spiritual views.

Raymond's story begins in the mid-1980s when he moved to Toronto, Ontario, into a brand-new condominium in the heart of the city. "I moved in first and was alone there for about two weeks before my partner and another roommate joined me. So I saw the spirit first," says Raymond. It happened a few times. Out of the corner of his eye, Raymond caught sight of a young male, about 5'6", walking through the house. "In fact," Raymond says, "the man was about my partner's height and the first time it happened, I thought he had somehow arrived early to surprise me." He followed the figure into the bedroom, but no one was there.

His partner Jim moved in next, but Raymond did not tell him of the unusual sighting. Jim worked at home and spent a lot of time in the house alone. Before long, he reported to Raymond that he too had seen something. He described the same thing: fleeting glimpses of a young male of medium height.

A few weeks later, Mary moved in. Raymond and Jim agreed not to say anything about the strange sightings because they were heading off on a trip to Alberta and didn't want to alarm their new housemate. "When we got back," recalls Raymond, "Mary asked if I came into her room the previous night. I said, 'No, why?' She told me she woke up and thought I was standing at the end of her bed. Then we fessed up and told her what we had seen. So we all knew. Okay, we have a ghost in the place. No big deal." That laissez-faire attitude would not last long.

Initially the spirit seemed content to meander about the house. Raymond says, "At night I would get this really strong sense of someone in the hall, and I was over-whelmed with curiosity. I would get up and wander around, try to speak to him, but he never appeared and never spoke to me." Jim often heard something moving in the pantry, but when he checked, nothing had shifted. Lights turned on in various rooms, and even the dogs seemed to sense the presence. They sat and watched as if someone was walking across the room. Visitors also claimed they saw someone in the apartment. Raymond says one guest described seeing a young man enter a room down the hall. These innocuous visits soon took a sinister turn.

One night Raymond woke to hear Mary screaming. Rushing to her room, he found her struggling in her bed. "It was like she was trying to push someone off her," says Raymond. "She said someone was trying to choke her." Shocked by the spirit's sudden violence, the trio agreed it was time to get rid of it. They hired a pair of paranormal experts to clear the house of whatever it was that coexisted there. But the man and wife team that arrived to perform the ritual surprised Raymond by saying they didn't sense anything malevolent. They thought perhaps Mary's experience may have just been a bad dream.

The ghost mediums agreed to continue with the cleansing and went down to Mary's room to begin the process. What happened next could well have been scalped from the pages of a spooky Hollywood screenplay. It took everyone, especially Raymond, by complete surprise.

"We were sitting in the living room, not sure what was going on, and I started to hyperventilate," Raymond recalls. "I'm not prone to hysteria so it was very weird. I started feeling like I was losing it. My neck went rigid. Jim and Mary got scared and called the couple. They came running and immediately said, 'Jason we know you're here.' My head whipped around, very *Exorcist*-like, and I had some awareness but it was clear he was part of me." Raymond doesn't know how the couple knew the spirit's name, but for the next three hours they spoke to the entity named Jason through Raymond, learning about his life and, more importantly, his death.

They learned that as a young boy, Jason lived on a farm, and one day while home alone with his brother, he had been playing around a well and somehow fell down it. Knowing his brother was watching him from a window, Jason lay there for a short while, conscious and anticipating his brother's help. His brother never came. Jason lapsed into unconsciousness and died thinking his brother had done nothing to rescue him.

The mediums discovered that Jason still didn't understand that he was dead, so they tried to guide him toward the next plane using regression techniques that took him back to his funeral to convince him he had died. "That was weird," says Raymond, "because I could see it all."

Jason resisted moving on, but finally left almost as suddenly as he had arrived. "I felt him leave and go into the light," says Raymond. After the entity's departure, the group relayed what had transpired to Raymond. "Both Mary and Jim, total nonbelievers, said the facial expressions and speech were not *me*, but totally Jason." The mediums explained that for some reason, Jason had been attached to Raymond although they had no idea how long the spirit had followed him or why.

That night's events unnerved Raymond. He now had to integrate the experience into his "rational, scientist world," and consider the possibility of an afterlife. However, he admits that while the door opened to these concepts, he "didn't walk through." He decided that since he helped the spirit move on, that would be the end of it.

Not so.

Five years later, Raymond lived in a new place with a new partner. He also felt moved to start exploring different avenues of spiritual awareness. "I decided to look into channeling courses and found one that sounded interesting. The class began with a meditation, but I would lose it in the class. It was as if my consciousness was knocked out of me." The instructor noticed Raymond struggling and suggested that he sit in with a different instructor who specialized in channeling. The new teacher told Raymond, "There is a young boy hanging around you for some reason." This instructor, who didn't know Raymond's story, made contact with the boy. The message came through clearly and succinctly. "He said his name was Jason and that he came back to tell you that you don't have to die alone."

Those simple words affected Raymond profoundly. Recently diagnosed with a chronic, fatal illness, he had been grappling with the concept of his death. "I felt very alone and that I would die alone," says Raymond. "That's when I realized that Jason thought he died alone and that no one came to help him, that no one cared. He was connected to me to help me realize I could break through the illusion that I was unlovable and alone. His message was the last kick I needed to really start healing in this life. It put me on the road to therapy and health, forced me to open my mind and my heart. I had been closed and resisting this life. Jason cracked the shell."

That was more than a decade ago, and Raymond has had no further contact with Jason. Regardless, the effects of that one message linger. "I chose to see my disease as a gift that helps me keep my life in perspective," Raymond says. "And I also chose not to believe I was psychotic, but that I'd had a massive transpersonal psychic experience."

A Spirit Named Wahoo

John Ricci admits that as a child, he could not be categorized as passive or mild-mannered. He and his chums tore around the Italian district of Portland, Oregon, stirring up trouble and enjoying every minute of it. Angelic they were not.

When they were in third grade, the group hung around the grocery store run by Eddie McCarthy. At some point, Eddie starting calling John "Wahoo" though he never explained why he chose that unusual nickname. The other boys in the gang adopted the nickname too, perhaps because it sounded so odd. John finally asked Eddie why he called him Wahoo, and to his surprise, the store owner told him that was the name of John's guardian angel. In John's personal account in *Angel Country* by Ria Biley, he says he didn't know how to react and wondered if Eddie was just joking. "But I was eight years old, and still young enough not to question anything a grown-up told me. It never occurred to me that what he said was other than the truth."

John attended a Catholic school where children were routinely taught about guardian angels. One day the teacher asked her students, "Who has a guardian angel?" She expected them to reply that everyone did, but instead John hollered out that he had a guardian angel and it was an Indian called Wahoo. Unimpressed, the teacher gave him a smack while the rest of the class howled with laughter. Not long after that, John forgot about his supposed angel and got on with the business of growing up.

As an adult, John's attitude didn't change much. He continued to push the envelope, so to speak, and developed a bad reputation. He admits he survived on "good luck" because he certainly moved in rough circles. But was it luck, or was it his guardian angel Wahoo?

During a visit to a family's gravesite, John heard a voice in his head that made him pause and rethink the idea of guardian angels. The voice, distinctly Aboriginal in nature, told him, "Don't go back." That may sound cryptic, but John knew exactly what the message meant. He teetered on the edge of making a decision that would alter his entire life, and when he heard those few words, he opted to move in a new direction. The result improved his life immensely—he met the woman he would eventually marry, became financially secure, had a family and even survived a life-threatening heart attack and open-heart surgery. As the years passed, John enjoyed the richness of his life and again forgot about Wahoo. Wahoo, however, did not so readily abandon John.

Though the circumstances of John's life ran smoothly, he still held on to some dubious business practices that gave him an unsavory reputation. When he saw an opportunity to make a lot of money by purchasing an old nursing home off a gambler who needed to divest the property quickly, John moved in for the kill. He planned to turn out the 17 nursing home residents and turn a big profit by renovating the building into apartments. Although the residents had nowhere to go and already lived in horribly underfunded conditions, John remained tantalized by the money he'd make. That's when Wahoo stepped in.

Wahoo's voice roused John from a deep sleep one night to admonish him. "Don't turn your back on those people. You can't throw them out. You have to take care of them." John knew he had to listen to the message, but thought at first that he might still be able to follow through with his original plan. He would simply wait until the state found somewhere else to house the nursing home residents.

That never happened. John instead took on the job of running the nursing home, and after a short while became enamored with the work. To his own surprise, he found he actually liked caring for the elderly. He ended up operating the business for 17 years, and by the time he retired he had added a second nursing home to his holdings. When he stopped to think about what an odd turn his life had taken, he thanked Wahoo for the guidance.

Naturally, the shift from bad-boy entrepreneur to altruist caught the attention of John's colleagues. They couldn't resist giving him the new nickname "Boy·Scout." The name tickled John so much that he dug out an old photograph of himself wearing his Boy Scout uniform at age 14. He enlarged the picture and hung it on the wall in his office.

Some time later, while chatting with one of the nursing home's suppliers, John got into a conversation about guardian angels. He shared the story about his guardian angel, a Native American named Wahoo. The man looked intently at the Boy Scout photo and said, "I see you've got a picture of him too." Confused, John followed the man's gaze to the spot on the wall and took a closer look at the picture. Suddenly, he saw exactly what the man referred to: in the background of the picture, by John's left foot, stood a dark-skinned man wrapped in a buffalo robe. As John stared at the picture, Wahoo's voice rang in his ear. "Didn't you know I was here?"

Synchronicity or Spirit Guide?

A guardian angel or spirit guide does not always make itself visible. Some people recognize their guardian spirits when they sense a protective energy nearby. In other cases, as in this story, the guiding force comes as an intuition, a barely formed thought that propels the recipient to take unusual actions. Is that just coincidence or is it guidance? Those in support of the latter theory say that in almost all cases, our guardian spirits bring some type of message from beyond to which we should pay close attention. We may receive such messages in an incredibly diverse number of ways, from dreams or signs to telepathic communication. Do inexplicable urges that run counter to our nature qualify? I leave that to you to decide.

Matthew Didier recalls an experience that took place "many, many, many, many years ago when I was young, foolish, had long black hair, and was still in high school. I'm now pushing 40." At that time in his life, he liked to hang out at clubs with a close group of friends. Though his friends generally considered Saturday to be their regular night to head out on the town, Matthew received a rare invitation to his favorite after-hours club on a Friday night. The date is permanently etched in his memory. "It was Friday December 7. I was pumped and ready to go," Matthew recalls.

Excited about the night ahead, Matthew spent extra time primping and preening. "I did my hair, did my makeup—it was the early eighties and I was a YOUNG teenager!" He donned his best clothes in anticipation of a rendezvous with a girl he hoped might join the group. Finally ready, he practically ran out of the house. "I bid adieu to my long-suffering father and mother and headed out the door." But his flight inexplicably halted just steps outside the front door.

"For no real reason," Matthew remembers, "I never made it off the first landing of the stairs, just outside the front door of our house. I stopped. I was not feeling sick or tired, and as a matter of fact, I was looking forward to the evening in hopes of spending some quality time with friends and this particular girl I had a severe crush on." Even so, he tuned into feelings that felt odd to him at that stage in his life. Matthew says his mind flooded with thoughts such as, "I really don't *want* to go and I don't *have* to go." So he turned on his heels, went back into his house, marched upstairs, showered, removed all the "glop" he had applied earlier and went to bed, despite not being at all tired.

Less than an hour after closing his bedroom door, Matthew's mother screamed in terror. Matthew ran downstairs to find his father suffering a major heart attack. He was pronounced dead just after midnight.

In retrospect, Matthew wonders about his abnormal decision to stay home. "Had I gone to that club, I probably would have arrived home at about 8 AM if I was lucky, not knowing anything and probably suffering from a few ill effects from the night before. Instead, I was home for my family, well rested, and more or less coherent to deal with the emergency and the ensuing grief."

Was that a form of guardian angel assistance? Matthew still isn't sure. "I've always found that evening *very* peculiar as it was not like me back then to choose to stay home and sleep instead of going out and being with friends, especially when I was honestly excited for the evening. Like I said, no angel appeared to me, nor any voice in my head, or real divine intervention, just a weird and uncommon change of heart and change of plans that spared me many issues and allowed me to be there, if I was needed, during that awful time for my family."

Guardian Voice

A voice inside your head shouts "Stop!" and triggers a life-saving reaction. Or it whispers "Yes," when you see that perfect gift, which turns out to be just what a friend needed, even if she didn't know it. Those who listen to these inner voices will tell you this is not an outburst of a chaotic mind or a random synaptic short circuit, but guidance from a spiritual place. Many believe that if we take time to tune in and pay attention, we might hear messages meant to guard or guide us safely through life.

Esther Supernault knows the voice in her head well. "I really think this is the voice of my guardian angel. I hear a young man. He is always very cheerful; it's a laughing voice. I hear that voice once in a while and it usually warns me."

Esther had her most recent experience with the voice in November 2003, while combing her hair in the bathroom. As she looked in the mirror, she suddenly saw a deep gash in her head. The vision expanded to reveal a "really messy cut" that looked as if shattered glass was embedded in her skull.

"Blood was pouring down my head and the voice said, 'You'll get this today,'" Esther recalls. She blinked hard to erase the horrifying image, which took a long time to fade. Esther took it seriously as some kind of warning, but couldn't decipher its exact meaning.

After the traumatizing sight of her bleeding skull, Esther drove into town with her seven-year-old granddaughter to buy new shoes for a night out at the ballet.

That night, they both dressed up for the theater and prepared to drive into the city, but the winter weather proved inhospitable. "As I backed out of the driveway, it was snowing like crazy and the temperature was just perfect for slippery road conditions," says Esther. As if to emphasize that point, their car slid through the first intersection they encountered. As Esther continued to slowly make her way to the highway, her granddaughter asked from the back seat, "Are we going to make it?"

Conditions had worsened when they reached the highway, and Esther remembered the ominous message in the bathroom that morning. "No ballet is worth having an accident," she says, "so we finally turned around and came back home." They discovered The Toy Castle ballet on television and accepted that as their consolation for staying home.

A few days later, still plagued by the image in the bathroom, Esther meditated and asked her guardian spirit if she would have received the head injury had she not turned back. The reply floored her. Her guardian spirit answered that yes, she would have suffered both head and internal injuries from an accident. Her granddaughter, though, would have lost both legs and may not have survived.

Esther says she now receives premonitions more regularly. She has worked hard to open herself to her guardian spirit's messages and she frequently dreams that something will go wrong with her vehicle or that an accident will happen. "I started paying attention so I could prevent them," she says.

Esther first started hearing the voice of her guardian spirit more than 25 years ago when she lived with her husband, son and newborn daughter. "She was very colicky, and I was depressed," Esther remembers. "I was really down so one day I went for a walk to a nearby schoolyard to get some fresh air. It was the weekend and no one was around. I just sat there by a snow-covered water fountain wondering what to do." As Esther fretted about her life, questioning why she should continue living so unhappily, she heard the voice for the first time. It said, "No, Esther, you have lots to do yet." She spun around to see the man who spoke to her, but found herself alone. Even so, the cheery male voice eased her melancholy. "I got up and walked home and got on with my life," says Esther. "That's when I decided to go into nursing."

It was eight years before she heard the voice again. This next occasion represented another crucial moment in Esther's life. One winter night, she was leaving her house for a class at the university, where she was working on her psychology degree. "I had some fish bones that I didn't want to leave in the house in case our dog found them, so I took them with me." She drove down the snowy, narrow country road and as it was getting dark, stopped by a slough to throw the bones away. "And as I tossed them, I felt my wedding ring go with them. I heard a 'ping', but couldn't see a thing. I mean, I was out in the middle of a prairie road after dark!" Esther ventured into the deep snow drifts to try to find her ring but realized the futility of her effort. "I remember standing in front of the truck in the headlights, crying because I had lost the beautiful ring my husband gave me. I literally cried out, 'Help me! I don't want to leave this spot until I find my ring because it is something special.' And that's when I heard the voice."

This time the voice offered directions: "Walk 10 steps ahead and three to your right." Without thinking, Esther followed the command. She looked down but couldn't see anything. She turned around. There, just two inches from the toe of her boot, her ring sparkled in the truck's headlights. She picked it up and put it back on her finger, then went into shock over what had happened. She couldn't believe it was actually her ring.

"What are the odds?" she still questions today. She drove to her university class too dazed to even dim her high beams. When she told her classmates of the incident, they didn't believe her. "It took me weeks to convince myself," she says.

Several years later, Esther lost her ring again during a summer evening volleyball game in a brush-enclosed area on her property. She had been playing for some time when she noticed that her ring no longer adorned her finger. "I freaked out. Everyone helped me look but we couldn't find it. It was getting dark and I thought I would ruin the party if I kept it up, so I dropped the search." But she didn't drop her will to find the ring. At home in bed that night, Esther asked her guardian spirit where it was. Just as she fell asleep she heard the words "It's on the boards."

The next day, she found the ring sitting on a pile of weathered gray boards piled near the volleyball area. "It was just sitting there, on the top board. And again I thought, 'How odd!' My neighbors thought I'd made it all up and were mad at me for making them search through the heavy brush."

Esther now knows her guardian angel more intimately. "I know his name. He is Native and though I haven't seen him, I could draw his picture. I know that we've had a past life together. He is here in this life to watch over me and help me out." She says that her Ojibwa roots, inherited from her grandmother, have helped her create a deeper spiritual connection with her guardian angel to the point where she has even dreamed of him attending her death. "I'm in my 80s and he comes and holds out his hand and tells me, 'Finally I can come for you.' In the dream I take his hand and everything goes black and all I can hear is a heart beating. Then I wake up."

Esther agreed to allow her stories to be published because she feels they can comfort people with the knowledge that guardian spirits exist to guide and guard us. "I think anything that wakens people to their own guardian angels is a good thing."

6
Angels Among Us

❦

"We not only live among men, but there are airy hosts, blessed spectators, sympathetic lookers-on, that see and know and appreciate our thoughts and feelings and acts."

— Henry Ward Beecher,
Royal Truths

❦

Protective Chinese Master

Where do we draw the line between coincidence and spiritual guidance? Some would argue that there are no coincidences. One must wonder, though, if it was a simple random occurrence that brought Sara to live in the district from which her guardian spirit originated.

Sara began to notice odd occurrences in her home in Los Angeles in the early 1990s. The sound on her stereo would suddenly blast at full volume even though no one was near the machine. The television channels changed before her eyes as she watched a program. The dishwasher started on its own. One day, she came home to find all the cushions on the sofa completely rearranged; instead of lying flat so someone could sit on them, they stood vertically.

After that, Sara felt the need for some sort of paranormal assistance. She brought in "ghost experts" to contact whatever spirit might be causing the disturbances. The paranormal team brought a Ouija board, and through it contacted an old Chinese master named Dong Wei from the Sai Kung district of Hong Kong. After communicating with the spirit, the paranormal team assured Sara it was a good spirit who would protect her. At the time, Sara found the information interesting, but had no intentions of moving to Hong Kong.

But as fate would have it, ten years later, Sara found herself moving into a tiny, ancient Chinese village house in the area of Sai Kung. She sent her story to Jeff Belanger's Ghostvillage.com online forum and announced, "As I write this now, I just heard what sounded like a dresser drawer opening upstairs, except no one is up there. The dogs also just opened their eyes." Ever since she moved in, the lights in the living room have flickered and dimmed on their own. At first, Sara thought the old wiring might be to blame, but she says, "My bulbs have never burned out and I have lived here for two years." Several of her friends have also witnessed this phenomenon.

What bothers her more is that the sound on her television and stereo still scares her by suddenly blasting at full volume. "I go to turn it down and it turns right back up again." And now, on top of that, her new DVD player seems to be part of the game; it turns itself on and plays "what it wants, whenever it wants." She hoped it might be some sort of mechanical fault and called a repairman. He inspected the machine thoroughly and put in several different discs. The machine worked perfectly every time. "He opened up the machine and said it was fine. Ugh!"

Could Dong Wei be trying to get Sara's attention for some reason? Or is her ancient Chinese master simply intrigued with modern luxuries?

A Bicycle Built for Two

The joy of freewheeling around on a bike brings a telling smile to the lips of anyone who knows the wind-tearing, rollicking energy that comes with conquering steep, rocky paths, jumping brooks and narrowly missing obstacles. There are times though, when in the thrill of the ride we forget how vulnerable our bodies are to the inevitable spills. A young rider I'll call Okie for this story considers himself more than just lucky to survive his risky ride. He is certain a guardian spirit literally plucked him from danger's path to save his skin.

As a young daredevil, Okie says he and his friends often ripped around the neighborhood on their BMX bicycles, in a competitive game of bike-tag. One day they were in their schoolyard doing just that, but the game ran long and Okie realized he should call it a day and head home. "Being a daredevil and not so bright," he says, "I decided to ride my bike down this hill."

The hill was actually an extension of the school yard. The grassy playground stood on a plateau, and beyond it a steep ridge dropped toward a path and creek. This would be no ordinary ride, however. Okie planned to make the trip without the use of his hands. He started out well but soon lost control. He recalls, "As I was picking up speed and heading towards the drop-off point, my bike began to wobble. Wobble, wobble, wobble. Just as I was about to crash and burn, it felt like I was lifted up off my bike." As if someone picked him up by his underarms and placed him on the ground, Okie landed

Okie and his friends often ripped around the neighborhood on their BMX bicycles, in a competitive game of bike-tag.

on his feet. The next thing he knew, he was standing behind his BMX. "I remember seeing my bike go for another 15 to 20 feet before falling over and sliding down the hill.

"Now, this is as clear as I remember it," Okie acknowledges. "Time could have fogged my memory of the event. But I still remember this feeling of being lifted up and placed, as you would place a chess piece for instance, out of harm's way."

Who might have protected the adventurous rider from a terrible tumble? Okie thinks that answer is obvious. "My mother had passed away recently, so I related it to her watching over me." No matter who or what helped him, however, Okie remains certain that he was saved from himself.

Sally the Bus Angel

"This story is true. I will swear to it until the day I go six feet under and cross over to the other side." So begins Rob's account of one of the most remarkable experiences of his life—a road trip with his guardian angel. This story originally appeared on castleofspirits.com.

Rob's youth was full of tumultuous times. His parents' marriage dissolved, and in the ensuing divorce he ended up living in Idaho with his father. As often happens in such situations, he was shuttled back and forth between parents for visits. On this occasion, he was taking the bus to Iowa to visit his mother, stepfather and sister. His father drove him to the bus station, made sure he found the right bus, helped him stow his suitcase and gave Rob a reassuring good-bye hug. "At the time I was 11 years old and very insecure about going such a long distance by myself," says Rob.

Rob climbed up the bus steps and made his way down the aisle to his seat. He barely had time to sit down and get comfortable when the person sitting next to him started up a conversation. The pale, dark-haired young woman introduced herself as Sally. She told Rob she lived in a suburb outside of New York City. After chatting for a few minutes, they discovered they were traveling the same route with the same connections and stopovers. Rob recalls, "She seemed friendly enough and so we talked the entire way back to Iowa."

As often happens when strangers meet en route, Rob found himself sharing much of his recent life history with Sally. She listened as he told her about the divorce, about traveling between the two cities to visit his mother and about his fears of traveling alone. "Throughout the entire ordeal she comforted me and kept me company, often letting me put my head in her lap to go to sleep," says Rob.

Many hours later, their journey finally ended. As the bus pulled into the terminal in Iowa, Rob saw his family huddled on the sidewalk, waiting for him. Excited now, Rob rushed to be first off the bus and ran to hug his mother. Still wrapped in his mother's arms, he saw Sally alight from the bus. "She gave me a smile and a wink, and walked into the bus station. I told my mom she had to meet the girl who helped me out on the trip."

Rob dragged his mother into the station, hurrying to catch up with Sally. He still recalls his shock upon entering the small, one-room building. "She was nowhere in sight. I asked the lady at the counter if someone matching Sally's description had walked in within the last few minutes, and she said no one had walked in at all."

To the left of the desk stood a cluster of pay phones, all empty. To the right of the counter stood the men's and women's washrooms. A woman emerged from the washroom and Rob asked her if she had seen anyone matching Sally's description in the bathroom with her. The woman replied that she had been the only person using the washroom, and walked away. There were no other exits or entrances to the station. Rob scanned the area for anyone walking away that looked like Sally, but there was no one within sight. Sally had just disappeared.

That may have been the end of it, and Rob might have reasoned that someone waiting in a car had whisked Sally away, had it not been for one little discovery. "Later, I looked at a detailed map of the New York area and found that the suburb Sally claimed to be from did not exist," explains Rob. "I am fully convinced that I was watched over on my bus trip by a guardian angel, and no one will ever convince me otherwise."

A Warning Knock

The minute Luana Houston moved into her house she knew a spirit lived within its walls. "You could hear squeaking floors, especially at night. It sounded like someone was walking around," she told me. "But I would check and find nothing. It happened several times, to the point where I got scared."

It was 1977 and Luana had two children to worry about. Her younger son Bill didn't appear to be affected, but her daughter Rae-ann attracted the spirit's attention. "The hustle and bustle was always around Rae-ann's room," says Luana. "The spirit was definitely attached to her." Luana realized this one night when the house's regular nocturnal creaking sounded like footsteps coming up the stairs. Frightened, she explored the darkened house and saw a light on in her daughter's room. Thinking, with some relief, that it was merely Rae-ann prowling about, Luana returned to her bed.

This happened a few times before Luana concluded her daughter was having trouble sleeping. Then one morning Rae-ann asked her, "Why do you keep coming into my room and turning on the light? You know I prefer to sleep with all the lights off." Dumbfounded, Luana chose not to say anything for fear of alarming her daughter. "Instead, I told a friend about it a while later," she says. Although the spirit's presence frightened her, she gradually got used to it.

As years passed, the spirit sporadically made noises to remind Luana of its presence. One year, the Houstons cut down a tree in the backyard, "and that caused a hullabaloo in the basement, with groans, weird noises and lights going on and off." At one point Luana confronted the man who sold her the house, demanding to know what kind of dwelling he unloaded on her. "He admitted that he had the same trouble," says Luana. The activity continued in Rae-ann's room. Objects would be moved around, lights turned on and off by themselves. Eventually she came to think of the spirit as her friend.

The unknown entity's attachment to Rae-ann persisted subtly until the year she met her first boyfriend. Luana says Rae-ann fell madly in love with a police officer who ended up renting out the basement suite of their house. One evening, Rae-ann had taken her university books downstairs to study while her boyfriend worked a late shift. Luana recalls, "I heard someone knocking on the door down there, and remember thinking it was odd that I hadn't heard anyone open the door or go down the stairs." A short time later, Rae-ann emerged from the basement, pale and shaken. Luana says, "She asked if I had gone down and knocked on the door, and accused me of playing a trick on her. But I told her I also heard the knocking."

Rae-ann said that after hearing the knock, her boyfriend's two dogs walked over to the door, tails wagging. That alone was unusual because they generally barked when someone arrived at the door. Rae-ann then got up to see who was there, but when she opened the door, she saw no one.

The next day, Rae-ann learned that her boyfriend had not worked a late shift as he claimed, but had worked on his moves with another woman at a local country music dance bar. She realized the knock on the door came while her unfaithful partner was out carousing. "She was devastated," Luana remembers, "but she felt sure that the spirit came to warn her."

Rae-ann eventually moved out and married, and Luana says it doesn't appear that the spirit followed her. Perhaps it simply needed to guide her through that first heartbreak to see her safely on her way.

Lost at the Beach

Imagine a hot summer day on a long, crowded beach on the shore of Lake Huron, Michigan. A little girl, preoccupied with her own imaginative game, looks around and does not recognize any familiar landmarks. The throngs of people around her suddenly seem unwelcoming and strange. Kelly Dyer still remembers being a lost seven year old unable to find her parents. Even more vivid is her recollection of the strangers who rescued her— strangers she believes were her guardian angels.

Kelly's family, including her grandparents, went to the beach en masse to escape the summer's blistering heat. Kelly remembers "tons of people on the beach." Everyone had migrated to the one place that might provide respite from the soaring temperatures. Bored of the adult company, Kelly wandered off to amuse herself. After a time, she looked up and discovered the landscape no longer looked familiar. "I realized I was lost," she told me in an interview. "I was crying as I walked along. I tried to look at everybody but no one looked like my grandma or my mom. In fact, I didn't realize I was quite turned around. I thought I was walking toward my family and in fact I was walking away from them."

To make matters worse, people kept approaching Kelly to ask her if they could help her find her way. Growing up in Michigan, Kelly says her mother always warned her to beware of strangers, particularly anyone offering candy or enticements. "I ran crying from these people because they were strangers, when they were just trying to help me," she recalls.

Out of the blue, a tall older gentleman accompanied by a woman approached Kelly. "I walked right up to them," she says. "The man was like my grandfather. He resembled him quite strongly, and the woman resembled my mother. She was the same age and size and had similar features." The man looked down at the frightened girl and said, "Would you like a piece of gum?" He pulled a stick of chewing gum from his jacket pocket. It was the same kind her grandfather used to offer her, and this man kept it in the same breast pocket. Despite the warnings about accepting such gifts from strangers, Kelly felt strangely comfortable and took the gum.

The elderly man put the gum back in his pocket and then told Kelly, "I'll take you to your parents. I know where they are." Kelly still finds her response odd. "For some reason, I said, 'Okay.' " Then, the man did something even more astonishing. "It was odd, but he just put me up on his shoulders, just like my grandfather did, and I wasn't afraid of him."

The couple turned around and headed in the opposite direction to that in which Kelly had been traveling. "They didn't ask along the way what my parents looked like," says Kelly. "They didn't ask for directions. They just walked right there. Along the way they got me laughing. The man sang songs like my grandfather did."

Atop the man's shoulders, Kelly relaxed. "I knew I was okay because they gave me a sense of comfort. I just knew they were going to take me back to my parents." Soon, they approached the picnic table where Kelly's family sat, anxiously wondering where she might be. "My parents were ecstatic to see me." The couple told Kelly's family they had found her about a mile down the beach, and her parents briefly turned their attention to Kelly to both scold and hug her. When they turned around to thank the couple for bringing her back, the man and woman were nowhere to be seen.

"They just disappeared," says Kelly. "They were standing right there, and then they were gone. My parents don't believe in that stuff, but my dad admits we should have been able to see them walking away because we were in an open area."

Kelly says her parents still don't believe she was rescued by guardian spirits, but Kelly knows it was more than a random act of a couple of Good Samaritans. Over her lifetime she has encountered several spirits, and this memory resonates in her mind as a sure sign that she is being looked after.

Angel Feathers

"I am a happening sort of person who seems to have a habit of encountering perilous situations. My guardian angel has a tough time of it!" That's how Rose-Marie Gower of North Wales sums up her incredible experiences. The most recent incident involves a never-ending supply of feathers and fits right in with all her other "weird and wacky" experiences.

She believes she encountered her first guardian angel in 1950 when she was just three months old. Rose-Marie's health failed in those first months, as she suffered from a violent intolerance to milk. She screamed day and night without reprieve; her family's nerves frayed to the breaking point. Then one night, while her grandmother held her and walked the floor in attempts to soothe her, Rose-Marie suddenly stopped crying. She actually remembers looking at the ceiling and seeing a white light and "the most beautiful face I have ever seen." Transformed, she smiled. Her grandmother sensed that Rose-Marie had seen an angel. From that time forth, she thrived.

At age 11, Rose-Marie gave her guardian angel another compelling reason to take action. During a summer holiday on the Isle of Guernsey off the coast of France, she decided to go fishing, and she chose a dangerous location on the rocks where the rough tides could easily cut off access to the island if one didn't pay close attention. In her efforts to catch a fish, Rose-Marie moved farther from shore, hoping to find a place where the fish were biting. Intent on bringing home dinner, she failed to notice that the tide had moved in and surrounded her rock. She realized she would have to jump a four-foot gap to reach safe soil.

"Falling into the water was not an option I cared to contemplate, as I would have been swept away. I was beginning to panic when suddenly a man materialized in front of me, seemingly from nowhere, and without a word carried me across the gap," Rose-Marie wrote in an article about her experience. Then her rescuer vanished without a word. She thought it odd, but her relief propelled her to run for her bicycle and ride home as fast as her legs could pedal. Rose-Marie never told her parents of the close call, but always wondered if that man was her guardian angel.

Her latest angel experience began in early 2004, when Rose-Marie saw a television show about angels. The guest on the show suggested that viewers could ask the angels for feathers as proof of their existence. At the time, Rose-Marie dismissed the thought as nothing more than a fanciful notion. However, the idea returned on her daily walk. "Nothing ventured, nothing gained," she thought, and said aloud, "Okay, if there is an angel in the vicinity, prove it!"

She rounded the bend in the road and saw that fluffy white feathers lay every few yards down the stretch until the road branched into a T-junction. Rose-Marie didn't collect any feathers until she returned later for her second daily walk. She says, "I picked up the only remaining feather and clutched it in my hand, meaning to take it home. On opening my palm, it had vanished. There was no wind and I swear it had not blown away."

She rounded the bend in the road and saw that fluffy white feathers lay every few yards down the stretch.

Rose-Marie mentioned this extraordinary occurrence to her husband, fully expecting a teasing response. "I was not disappointed. With tongue firmly imbedded in cheek, he asked any passing angel to send him a sign." Later, as he turned down the duvet, he found two white, fluffy feathers on their bed. "We do not have feather pillows or duvets," Rose-Marie points out.

The feathers kept appearing. The following morning, several white feathers blew around the patio outside. Rose-Marie's husband found a feather by his place setting at the breakfast table. Inside his car, feathers lay on the driver's seat and on the floor by the pedals. The feathers continued to turn up in very unexpected places.

After telling several friends about the mysterious replicating feathers, Rose-Marie heard from several people who also experienced remarkable results. She received this message via e-mail from a good cyber-pal in Florida: "Last night before going to bed I asked with all seriousness for an angel to send me a feather. Well, I woke up this morning covered in feathers. I have two feather pillows on my bed and the seam had come apart on one. Feathers were everywhere. The seam was not ripped; the thread was just gone and all the stuffing came out during the night. I have a ceiling fan that picked up the feathers. They were swirling through the air and landing on the furniture only to be picked up and swirled around again. It looked like a fluffy snow-storm. I had to turn off the fan and I spent about 30 minutes or so vacuuming up all the feathers. I will never again ask for an angel feather. There is an old saying: 'Be careful what you ask for because you might get it.' I got it all right."

Rose-Marie says even skeptics found the challenge too hard to resist. After posting her story on a website, she received a scathing response, not unexpected, from one of the posters on that forum. However, a few days later she received a contrite apology from the fellow. He admitted that he asked the angels for feathers as a joke, only to find several in his car that were not there before. There seemed no way that they could have arrived there by natural means.

Despite the continuing arrival of feathers and evidence from others, Rose-Marie is not convinced angels are sending them. "I think the feathers are probably no more than an amazing set of coincidences, but it gives one pause for thought!"

The Power of Friendship

In the spring of 1976, David Williams was a farmer and "back to the lander," living with his wife and two young sons on British Columbia's Saltspring Island. Like many other idealistic young people of the '60s, he had given up a promising professional career at Simon Fraser University in Vancouver to return to a more organic way of life. Looking back, he says, "This was in the belief that it might provide inspiration for others who thought, for one reason or another, that societal transformation was necessary." Little did he know that it would also lead to a transformative spiritual experience, one of the most supernatural encounters of his life.

The hard physical work of farming built his character and strong physique, but did not bring in much money. If a subsistence farmer wanted to enjoy any extras like books or the occasional trip off-island, he had to find other sources of income. Consequently, David occasionally worked for two friends named Joe and Dennis who ran a small construction business.

One very cold April morning, David met Joe and Dennis at the site where they were building a second-story addition to a house over a carport. That day, they planned to put in pre-formed roof trusses and strap them securely in place. David didn't mind heights and, being agile and strong, he volunteered to climb up with Joe to set the wooden frames in place. Once they set up the roof trusses, they fastened the strapping to them.

Thinking the job was complete, Joe suggested they hang out over the edge of the last truss while leaning on the overhanging strapping in order to fasten a heavy barge board in place.

"Now, this was an unconventional way of doing it to say the least," David says. "At the peak, where I stood, it was 25 feet down to a paved driveway." Still, this shortcut would save them time and the hassle of placing ladders or scaffolding and working up from the ground. "I had no reason to think that Joe and Dennis, much more experienced than me, didn't know what they were doing. After all, no matter how informal and friendly our relationship was, they were still my bosses."

Joe and David each took an end of the barge board and, hammers in hand and lying on their bellies out over the drop, began slowly and with some difficulty to lift the board up into place. Once they lifted it, they could fasten it by driving in the nails they had already started.

They had barely begun when David felt a shift behind him. "Then, with increasing speed, I felt the whole roof structure tilt up behind us," he says. "Our combined weight had caused the light tacking at the rear to pull away from the main house and had now begun an irreversible process which catapulted Joe and me headfirst toward the pavement 25 feet below."

It seemed to David that everything happened in slow motion. "I never thought I would die. Merely that landing was going to hurt," he recalls. "Besides, this was springtime, I had a young wife and two children I adored and a farm to care for. I had to be indestructible. This was not a good day to die."

The need for self-preservation somehow took over as the ground rushed toward him. David knew he mustn't land on his head. As he fell, he rotated his body and finally, after what seemed like a long time, he landed on his feet. As his legs gave way under the impact, his outspread hands hit the ground, followed by his face. He lost consciousness for a fraction of a second, and when he came to, he realized the whole roof assembly that had reared up behind them was falling on top of him and Joe. Something heavy landed on David's legs and pinned him to the ground. "I could hear moaning and a snuffling sound. I looked over at Joe, who lay under trusses and lumber. The sound was coming from him though all I could see of his head was blood. His head appeared to be the wrong shape."

Dennis scrambled down and yelled for the woman who owned the house to call the ambulance. He rushed over, asked David if he was all right, then hurried to Joe, who lay buried under heavy boards. Dennis began dragging the lumber off his friend. David freed himself and crawled over to Joe as well.

"Oh God, oh God. I never should have let him do it that way," Dennis said, looking utterly sick and bewildered. "He fell like a stone; he just fell straight down, right on to his head. He can't possibly live. Where is that bloody ambulance?"

David says, "Dennis had been a medic in World War II. I believe he had lived through Normandy and Holland as the Canadians fought their way to Germany, and had seen war and its consequences. That he was so distressed by the sight of Joe was pretty unnerving."

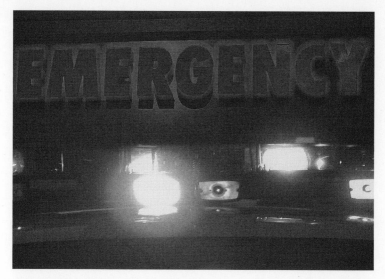

The dreadful sounds of Joe fighting for his life filled the ambulance as they drove.

It seemed like hours before the volunteer ambulance arrived, although David was later told it took only ten minutes. One of the young attendants looked at Joe, grimaced, turned to one side and vomited. The emergency workers quickly lifted Joe onto a stretcher and into the ambulance. Dennis helped David, who had injured his foot and appeared to be in shock, hobble over to the ambulance as well. David sat in the front seat beside the driver. The other attendant remained with Joe in the back. The dreadful sounds of Joe fighting for his life filled the ambulance as they drove.

At Lady Minto Hospital, the emergency room team immediately went to work on Joe. The hospital staff placed David in a wheelchair and rolled him into the hall. Within minutes, Joe's wife and 17-year-old daughter rushed in, having been summoned from their home in the town of Ganges by a phone call from Dennis. Frantic with worry, they rushed up to David and asked where Joe was and what was wrong with him.

David remembers. "Like a fool, I said, 'He's okay.' Then I began to cry, out of shock, I suppose, and sick dread that Joe was going to die and that they were going to have to bear it right there, right then. At that point, a nurse came out and took them aside into another room."

Not long after, Joe was wheeled out and into the ambulance again. His wife and daughter got into their car and followed the ambulance as it roared away, siren screaming, toward Fulford Harbor and the ferry to Victoria.

After an examination by his family physician, who diagnosed a broken big toe and a mild concussion, David was told he could go home. His wife Kate arrived to pick him up just as the emergency nurse who accompanied Joe to the ferry returned to the hospital. David knew the nurse fairly well, since Saltspring was a small community in those days, and he asked her about Joe. She replied that it didn't look like he would make it.

Back at home, David crawled gratefully into bed to recover. They put a cardboard box over his painful toe and he eventually settled in for a restless evening. Kate would sleep on the couch downstairs so as not to disturb his toe.

David felt overwhelmed by jumbled emotions: great fatigue combined with horror at what had happened to Joe and immense relief at being spared that same fate.

"Joe was a nice man," David reflects. "In fact, he was that and more. There wasn't a mean bone in his body. I was very fond of him and couldn't have wanted a better friend. I was filled with dread at the thought of what he had gone through and was probably experiencing at that moment. Nevertheless, I was also utterly exhausted, and soon fell asleep."

Later, David heard Kate preparing the boys and herself for bed downstairs. He heard her close the damper on the wood stove for the night and blow out the kerosene lamp. She called out good night, and he mumbled a response.

When David woke it was dark, the loft lit only by the moon and stars shining in the skylight above his bed. As his eyes adjusted to the light, he saw a figure standing next to him, watching him. David reached out, thinking Kate had come up to check on him. But no one was there.

Not long after, Kate called out to him, "Dave, are you awake?" He replied that he was and that he thought he had seen her standing beside the bed. Somebody had certainly been there, of that David was certain.

Kate said, "He was just here, too. He was standing right beside me."

"It must have been Joe," they said together.

"We both knew in that instant," David recalls, "without a shadow of a doubt, that Joe had come to see how I was and to say good-bye."

Several days later, June and Renee, Joe's wife and daughter, came to visit the Williams, and told David and Kate of a strange occurrence. After the first of a series of operations, Joe kept coming out of the anesthesia and asking, "Is Dave okay? Is Dave okay?" He seemed frantic with worry about his friend and whether he was badly hurt or even dead.

Based on June and Renee's information and from a call to the hospital, David surmised that as Joe underwent the operation and hovered near death that dreadful night, his concern for David was so strong that he came to check up on his friend himself.

The story ends with an unexpected positive twist. Joe survived his massive head injuries and, though he will likely always suffer the consequences of his accident, is still alive and well 28 years later. The incredible experience of witnessing a guardian spirit lives on in David.

"This is a true story," he says, "and I'll never forget it."

The End